GUINNESS WORLD RECORDS

EXTREME!

FUN FACTS & ACTIVITIES

D1307214

AMERICAN
EDUCATION
PUBLISHING™

American Education Publishing™
An imprint of Carson-Dellosa Publishing LLC
Greensboro, North Carolina

Due to the publication date, the facts and figures contained in this book are current as of August 24, 2011.

©2012 Guinness World Records Limited

Visit Guinness World Records at
guinnessworldrecords.com

Carson-Dellosa Publishing LLC
P.O. Box 35665
Greensboro, NC 27425 USA

ISBN 978-1-60996-893-9   01-153121151

Photo: Guinness World Records Limited

Photo: Guinness World Records Limited

WHAT'S INSIDE?

Photo: Guinness World Records Limited

CAUTION CAUTION CAUTION

A Note to the Reader of This Book

Inside this book, you will find facts about unusual objects and creatures, epic journeys, and thrilling feats. Read and enjoy the stories, but never try to set a world record on your own! Breaking records can be dangerous and even life threatening. If you think you have a good idea for a safe, record-breaking event, talk to an adult. You can learn more about how to set a world record at guinnessworldrecords.com.

Throughout this book, you will find activity ideas that encourage you to learn more, get active, use your brain, be creative, and have fun. Try all the activities, but pause and think before you do each one. Ask yourself: What should I do to be safe and follow the rules? Do I need a parent's permission to go somewhere or to use materials? Always ask an adult if you are unsure.

Now, turn to any page. Get ready to be amazed by Guinness World Records® facts!

CAUTION CAUTION CAUTION

Photo: Guinness World Records Limited

EPIC ADVENTURES

Photo: Guinness World Records Limited

Smallest Model Sailing Boat (Radio-Controlled)

The smallest radio-controlled sailing boat measures 5 in. (15.2 cm) long, 2 in. (6.3 cm) wide, and 1 ft. 2 in. (35.6 cm) tall. It was built by Claudio Diolaiti in Nice, France, and was tested on November 14, 2007.

Photo: Guinness World Records Limited

Did You Know?
Sailboats have eight basic parts: hull, tiller, rudder, mainsail, mast, boom, jib, and keel.

ACTIVITIES

These squares are $\frac{1}{4}$-inch wide and $\frac{1}{4}$-inch tall. Use them to draw the smallest sailboat at $\frac{1}{4}$ scale. (Hint: Convert the boat's length and height to inches and divide by four. The answers will provide the measurements for your drawing.)

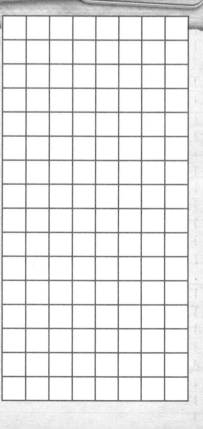

Fastest Skateboard Speed (Standing)

Photo: Guinness World Records Limited

The fastest skateboard speed from a standing position was 70.21 mph (113 km/h). The record was set by Douglas da Silva (Brazil) on October 20, 2007.

Did You Know?
The first outdoor skate park was constructed for skateboarders in Florida in 1976.

ACTIVITIES

1. Find out the speed limit on a highway near your home. How many miles per hour over that limit was da Silva traveling?

_____

2. How many miles per hour faster is an average race car (200 mph) than the fastest skateboard?

_____

3. Write your favorite way to roll down the street or sidewalk.

_____

Most Parachute Jumps in 24 Hours

Jay Stokes (USA) made 640 successful parachute jumps in 24 hours on September 8–9, 2006, in Greensburg, Indiana.

Photo: Guinness World Records Limited

Did You Know?

Free fall occurs after skydivers jump but before they release a parachute. Gravity speeds the diver toward maximum velocity.

ACTIVITIES

1. About how many jumps did Stokes make each hour? Round to the nearest tenth.

   _____

2. Which part of skydiving would you enjoy most: jumping out of the plane, free falling, or floating back to Earth under a parachute? Explain your answer.

   _____

   _____

Deepest Shipwreck

Photo: Guinness World Records Limited

In 1996, Blue Water Recoveries Ltd. (UK) used sonar to find the German World War II ship SS *Rio Grande* at the bottom of the South Atlantic Ocean. The wreck lies at a depth of 18,904 ft. (5,762 m).

Did You Know?

The find was confirmed using a remotely operated vehicle.

ACTIVITIES

Imagine a submarine observes these things as it descends to the ocean depths. Write them in order from shallowest to deepest.

vampire squid (10,000 feet) _____

tube worms (19,300 feet) _____

loggerhead turtle (10 feet) _____

SS *Rio Grande* (18,904 feet) _____

lanternfish (3,000 feet) _____

red algae (surface) _____

Fastest 1,000 Kilometers on a Jet Ski

Photo: Guinness World Records Limited

The fastest 1,000 km on a Jet Ski was 10 hours 9 minutes set by Juan Felix Bravo Aguilar (Spain) in San Martin de Valdeiglesias, Spain, on July 3, 2009.

Did You Know?
Spain has almost 5,000 mi. (8,046 km) of beaches.

CHECK THIS OUT!

How long do you think it would take you to drive from Detroit, Michigan, to New York City, New York? That is about the distance that Juan Felix Bravo Aguilar (Spain) traveled on a Jet Ski in just over 10 hours! During his 10-hour trek, he stopped only to refuel and to take on food and water.

For his attempt at the world record, a 1.24-mile course was set up for Aguilar. To finish the 1,000 kilometers, he had to complete the course 500 times. He averaged times between 2 minutes, 21 seconds and 2 minutes, 23 seconds per each completed lap. His fastest lap was 2 minutes 19 seconds. At times, Aguilar reached speeds of 70 miles per hour!

ACTIVITIES

1. Find Detroit, Michigan, and New York City, New York, on a map of the United States. To which city do you live closest? Estimate the number of miles between that city and yours.

_____

_____

2. There are 0.62 miles in a kilometer. How many miles did Aguilar complete during this 1,000-kilometer adventure?

   a. 62

   b. 620

   c. 6,200

   d. 6.2

3. What was Aguilar's average speed in miles per hour? Circle your answer.

   more than 60 mph   **less than 60 mph**

4. What does *trek* mean?

   a. journey

   b. swim

   c. sleep

   d. interrogation

5. Find the average of the following numbers: 4, 10, 8, 6, 7.

   _____

6. Aguilar completed the 1.24-mile course 500 times in about 10 hours. Complete the chart to show how many miles he had traveled at each hour mark.

Time in Hours	1	2	3	4	5	6	7	8	9	10
Mileage		124				372				

Most Arrows Caught by Hand in Two Minutes (Blindfolded)

Photo: Guinness World Records Limited

Anthony Kelly (Australia) caught two arrows in two minutes while blindfolded. The arrows were shot from a distance of 26.24 ft. (8 m).

Did You Know?
Kelly caught 30 in. (76 cm) wooden shaft arrows with steel tips.

ACTIVITIES

1. Put on a blindfold and have a friend toss a stuffed animal or a soft ball. How many times can you catch it? Trade places. Who caught the most objects while blindfolded?

_____

2. Stand 26 feet away from a friend. (Use a yardstick or tape measure to find the distance.) How many times can you throw and catch a soft ball from that far away?

_____

Whip Cracking (Longest Whip)

Photo: Guinness World Records Limited

The longest whip cracked was 216 ft. (65.83 m). It was used by Adam Winrich (USA) in Fall Creek, Wisconsin, on May 24, 2006.

Did You Know?
When a whip cracks, its tip makes a mini sonic boom as it travels above the speed of sound.

ACTIVITIES

1. Each story of a building is about 10 feet tall. If you stretched out the whip, about how many stories tall would it be? Round to the nearest whole number.

_____

2. Sound waves travel four times faster through water than they do through air. If sound travels at 767 miles per hour through air, how fast does it travel through water?

_____

Highest Wall Climb on Darts

Photo: Guinness World Records Limited

On November 11, 2009, Maiko Kiesewetter (Germany) reached a height of 16 ft. 5 in. (5 m) by climbing on darts.

Did You Know?

The first dartboards might have been cross sections of trees. The trees' rings may have inspired the rings on the modern dartboard.

ACTIVITIES

1. The word *dart* can be used as a noun and a verb. Write a definition for each word.

   dart (*n.*) _____

   dart (*v.*) _____

2. If pairs of darts were embedded in the wall every nine inches, how many pairs would be needed to reach 16 feet, 5 inches? Round to the nearest whole number.

   _____

Longest Platform-to-Platform Bicycle Jump

Photo: Guinness World Records Limited

In 2009, Vittorio Brumotti (Italy) jumped 13 ft. 2 in. (4.02 m) from platform to platform on a bicycle in Milan, Italy.

Did You Know?

One easy bike trick is the bunny hop. Pull up on the handlebars to lift the front tire. Use your legs to lift the back wheel.

ACTIVITIES

1. With a friend, leap on the floor from pillow to pillow. How far can you spread the pillows apart and still make the jump?

   _____

2. How far did Brumotti jump in inches?

   _____

3. If a bed mattress is 80 inches long, how many mattresses could Brumotti jump over? Round to the nearest whole number.

   _____

Tallest Tightrope Pyramid

Photo: Guinness World Records Limited

Wallenda Family Entertainment (USA) performed an eight-person, four-level pyramid on a tightrope 25 feet (7.62 m) above the ground in Kurashiki, Japan, on August 4, 2001.

Did You Know?

In 1859, Charles Blondin crossed the gorge below Niagara Falls on a tightrope 160 feet (50 m) above the water.

CHECK THIS OUT!

In August 2001, Wallenda Family Entertainment (United States) set a world record for the tallest tightrope pyramid. However, the Wallenda family is no newcomer to daring acts. The family has performed amazing high wire acts for over 100 years!

The family is also known as "The Flying Wallendas." The nickname came from a newspaper article written after a circus performance in the 1930s or 1940s, in which the wire slipped slightly as four family members were performing. Everyone fell to the wire, but no one was hurt. The next day, a reporter who witnessed the accident wrote in the newspaper, "The Wallendas fell so gracefully that it seemed as if they were flying." The headline read "THE FLYING WALLENDAS," and the nickname has remained to this day.

1. How many people were included in the Tallest Tightrope Pyramid?

   a. 4

   b. 8

   c. 25

   d. 100

2. Build a pyramid with blocks or upside-down paper cups. How many levels tall can you make your pyramid?

   _____

3. Do you think "The Flying Wallendas" makes sense as a nickname for this group? Explain why or why not.

   _____

   _____

4. Fill in this pyramid. Each number should equal the sum of the two numbers below it.

   21

   10   11   14   12

5. Pretend you were at the circus during which The Flying Wallendas eventually got their name. Write an article about the event that would appear in the newspaper the next day.

   _____

   _____

   _____

   _____

   _____

Largest Solar-Powered Boat

Photo: Guinness World Records Limited

The MS *Tûranor PlanetSolar* (Switzerland) is 101 ft. 8 in. (31 m) long. It is covered with 5,780 sq. ft. (537 m²) of solar panels.

Did You Know?

Nine solar plants in California's Mojave Desert make up the largest solar thermal power generating plant in the world.

ACTIVITIES

1. In full sunlight, set one ice cube on white paper and one ice cube on black paper. Which paper absorbs the most heat from the sun and makes the ice cube melt faster?

   _____

   _____

2. Would it be better to take a solar-powered boat trip during the summer or during the winter? Explain your answer.

   _____

   _____

Fastest Railed Vehicle (Rocket Sled)

Photo: Guinness World Records Limited

A four-stage rocket sled system reached a speed of 9,468 ft. (2,886 m) per second in 6.031 seconds at Holloman Air Force Base in New Mexico on April 30, 2003.

Did You Know?

The sled's speed was equivalent to 6,453 mph (10,385 km/h).

ACTIVITIES

1. At its top speed, how many feet could the rocket sled travel in six seconds?

   _____

2. There are 5,280 feet in a mile. How many miles could the sled travel in six seconds? Round to the nearest tenth.

   _____

3. How is the sled like a space rocket?

   _____

Most Consecutive Yoga Positions on a Motorcycle

Photo: Guinness World Records Limited

Yogaraj C P (India) performed 23 yoga positions while driving a motorcycle in Mumbai, India, on February 17, 2011.

Did You Know?
Yoga started in India over 5,000 years ago. It focuses on stretching, balancing, and breathing.

ACTIVITIES

Try these yoga poses:

Butterfly: Sit with the soles of your feet together. Hold on to your feet and drop your knees to the floor. Sit up tall.

Gorilla: Stand with legs wide. Bend forward from the waist, letting your arms hang down. Swing your upper body.

Airplane: Stand up tall. Reach your arms out from your shoulders. Tip forward and point one foot behind you in the air.

Which pose did you like best? Explain your answer.

Fastest Speed for a Car Driven Blindfolded

Metin Senturk (Turkey) drove a car unsighted at a speed of 182.03 mph (292.89 km/h) at Urfa airport in Turkey on March 31, 2010.

Photo: Guinness World Records Limited

Did You Know?
Senturk is president of the World Handicapped Foundation. He drove a Ferrari F430.

ACTIVITIES

Read the list of vehicles and their approximate speeds. Write them in order from slowest to fastest.

cruise ship (25 mph)   _____

high-speed train (187 mph)   _____

Senturk's car driven without sight (182 mph) _____

mountain bike (14 mph)   _____

car on highway (65 mph)   _____

space shuttle (17,320 mph)   _____

Fastest Time to Run 100 Kilometers on a Treadmill (Male)

Photo: Guinness World Records Limited

On November 28, 2004, Arulanantham Suresh Joachim (Australia) ran 100 km on a treadmill in a time of 7 hours 21 minutes 40 seconds in Ontario, Canada.

Did You Know?
Surveys have shown that 53% of runners are male and 47% are female.

CHECK THIS OUT!

Arulanantham Suresh Joachim (Australia) was born in a war-torn area, Jaffa, near what is now Tel Aviv, Israel. His childhood inspired him to work toward spreading peace and goodwill around the world.

Joachim first found out about Guinness World Records when he was 22 years old. He felt that getting into the record books would be a good way to gain the world's attention and promote his charitable ideas. His aim is to hold the most records in the world and to raise $1 billion for charity in the process. Among the records Joachim wants to break are driving a car backward for the furthest distance, running backward for the furthest distance, and riding a motorbike backward for the furthest distance. He also wants to run around the world, through 180 cities, in the shortest time while carrying a peace torch.

ACTIVITIES

1. What are two goals Joachim hopes to accomplish?

   1. _____

   2. _____

2. Which is not a record that Joachim wants to break?

   a. driving a car backward for the furthest distance

   b. running backward for the furthest distance

   c. making the most parachute jumps in 24 hours

   d. riding a motorbike backward for the furthest distance

3. What words can you make from the letters P-E-A-C-E and G-O-O-D-W-I-L-L?

   _____   _____

   _____   _____

   _____   _____

   _____   _____

4. Joachim hopes to run around the world, through 180 cities. How many U.S. cities can you name? List as many as you can.

   _____   _____   _____

   _____   _____   _____

   _____   _____   _____

   _____   _____   _____

   _____   _____   _____

5. Why is it important to give to charity?

   _____

   _____

Oldest Person to Climb Mt. Everest (Male)

Photo: Guinness World Records Limited

Min Bahadur Sherchan (Nepal) was 76 years 340 days old when he reached the highest point on Earth on May 25, 2008.

Did You Know?
Mt. Everest rises 29,029 ft. (8,848 m) above sea level. That's over five miles tall!

ACTIVITIES

1. Give your age in years and days.

_____

2. What is the highest point in the state or area where you live? How many feet does it reach above sea level?

_____

3. How does it make you feel to be high above the ground?

_____

Fastest Speed Barefoot Waterskiing (Female)

Photo: Guinness World Records Limited

Teresa Wallace (USA) water-skied without skis at a speed of 96.08 mph (154.63 km/h) at Firebird International Raceway in Chandler, Arizona, in 2006.

Did You Know?
Water-skiers use hand signals to communicate with the driver of the boat.

ACTIVITIES

1. Ordinary water-skiers reach speeds of 45 miles per hour. Barefoot skiing is often faster. How many miles per hour faster than a conventional water-skier is the fastest barefoot water-skier?

_____

2. Circle your favorite ways to speed through the water.

boogie boarding	**swimming**
surfing	**waterskiing**
boating	**body surfing**

Longest Marathon on a Roller Coaster

Photo: Guinness World Records Limited

Richard Rodriguez (USA) rode the Pepsi Max Big One and Big Dipper roller coasters at the Pleasure Beach in Blackpool, United Kingdom, for 405 hours 40 minutes in 2007.

Did You Know?

Most roller coaster cars don't have engines. They travel using gravity, friction, and speed.

ACTIVITIES

1. For about how many days did Rodriguez ride? Round to the nearest whole day.

   _____

2. Circle the name of a roller coaster you would like to ride.

   Mindbender (Alberta, Canada)

   Top Thrill Dragster (Sandusky, Ohio)

   Oblivion (Staffordshire, England)

   Eejanaika (Fujiyoshida, Japan)

Tallest Indoor Ice Climbing Wall

Photo: Guinness World Records Limited

An indoor climbing wall made of ice is in the O2 World Building in Seoul, South Korea. It stands 65 ft. 7 in. (20 m) tall.

Did You Know?

Ice climbers wear *crampons* (traction devices) on their feet. They kick into the ice, then swing an ax overhead to help them climb.

ACTIVITIES

1. Give the height of the tallest indoor ice wall in inches.

   _____

2. If each climbing step were 18 inches, how many steps would it take to climb the entire wall? Round to the nearest whole number.

   _____

3. If each 18-inch step took three minutes, how many hours would it take to reach the top of the wall?

   _____

Longest Duration Juggling Three Objects Blindfolded

Photo: Guinness World Records Limited

The longest duration juggling three objects blindfolded is 47.26 seconds and was achieved by Zdeněk Bradáč (Czech Republic) at the 20th International Record Festival in Pelhrimov, Czech Republic, on June 12, 2010.

Did You Know?
World Juggling Day is held each year on the Saturday closest to June 17.

CHECK THIS OUT!

Have you ever heard the saying, "If at first you don't succeed, try, try again"? Even world record holders may not be successful on their first tries, but, as another saying goes, "Practice makes perfect"!

During his first attempt to break the record of the Longest Duration Juggling Three Objects Blindfolded, the magician, juggler, and escapologist Zdeněk Bradáč (Czech Republic) was performing on stage during a festival on a hot June day. Unfortunately, Bradáč was unsuccessful because he lost concentration due to the hot weather. Luckily, he was offered another chance to perform in the shade. There, he broke his previous record of 25.30 seconds by more than 20 seconds. His perseverance really paid off!

1. How long did Bradáč juggle three objects blindfolded?

   a. 15.26 seconds

   b. 20 seconds

   c. 25.30 seconds

   d. 47.26 seconds

2. Draw a calendar for June of this year. Label dates correctly and include events that usually happen in June.

June						

3. Ask an adult to blindfold you as you get ready for bed at night. Then, complete the following activities without removing your blindfold. Which tasks were easy? Which tasks were difficult? Circle your answers.

Brushing your teeth	**easy**	**difficult**
Washing your face	**easy**	**difficult**
Putting on your pajamas	**easy**	**difficult**
Climbing into bed	**easy**	**difficult**

4. Write about a time when your first attempt at something was unsuccessful. Did you try again? Were you successful on your second (or third) attempt?

   _____

   _____

5. In your own words, explain the phrase "Practice makes perfect." Do you agree with this statement? Explain why or why not.

   _____

   _____

Photo: Guinness World Records Limited

Colin Furze (UK) created the longest motorcycle, presented in Leicestershire, United Kingdom, in 2008. It was 46 ft. 3 in. (14.03 m) long.

Did You Know?

Up to eight standard motorcycles can fit in a parking space designed for one car.

ACTIVITIES

1. If a standard motorcycle is six feet (72 inches) long, about how many standard motorcycles would it take to match the length of the Longest Motorcycle? Round to the nearest whole number.

_____

2. Imagine riding the world's Longest Motorcycle. What are some problems you might have driving through town?

_____

_____

Longest Time Breath Held Voluntarily (Male)

Photo: Guinness World Records Limited

Ricardo da Gama Bahia (Brazil) held his breath underwater for 20 minutes 21 seconds on September 16, 2010.

Did You Know?
Bahia hyperventilated with oxygen for 20 minutes 48 seconds before beginning the attempt.

ACTIVITIES

1. Twenty minutes is what fraction of one hour?

   _____

2. Humans breathe in air with oxygen and breathe out air with carbon dioxide. The chemical symbol for carbon dioxide is CO_2. What is the chemical symbol for oxygen?

   _____

3. Can you hold your breath for 15 seconds? Circle your answer.

   yes   **no**

Smallest Radio-Controlled Model Aircraft

John Wakefield (UK) created model BF5, a radio-controlled aircraft with a wingspan of just 2.72 in. (69 mm) on October 27, 2010.

Did You Know?
The aircraft flew for 6 minutes 56 seconds. It weighed just 0.07 ounces (1.98 g).

Photo: Guinness World Records Limited

ACTIVITIES

1. A *model* is a miniature representation of something. Describe a model you have made or would like to make.

_____

2. The model aircraft has a wingspan of about three inches. Is your index finger longer or shorter than three inches? Circle your answer.

longer   **shorter**

3. What other tiny things fly through the air?

_____

Most Consecutive Fire Flames Blown by Mouth (Without Refueling)

Photo: Guinness World Records Limited

Jitender "Jassy" Singh (India) blew 76 consecutive flames by mouth without refueling on the set of *Guinness World Records* in 2011.

Did You Know?

Fire breathers create a fireball by breathing a fine mist of fuel over a flame. An assistant with a fire extinguisher waits nearby.

ACTIVITIES

1. How many more flames would Singh need to blow for a 100-flame record?

   _____

2. Fire breathing is very dangerous, but can be done safely by trained professionals. Do you think fire breathing is something that should be done? Explain why or why not.

   _____

   _____

Most Cans Crushed With a Vehicle in Three Minutes

Photo: Guinness World Records Limited

Ian Batey, driving a monster truck for Burn Energy Drink (UAE), set the record for most cans crushed with a vehicle in three minutes. He crushed 61,106 cans in Dubai, United Arab Emirates, on March 6, 2010.

Did You Know?
A *monster truck* is a pickup truck modified or built with very large wheels and suspension.

CHECK THIS OUT!

What do you know about recycling? *Recycling* means "taking old items and making new products from them." Recycling is important for a number of reasons. It saves energy, saves Earth's resources, and reduces the amount of waste in landfills.

Several things can be recycled, including paper, glass, plastic bottles, and aluminum cans. In the United States, only 60 percent of aluminum cans are recycled. That means 40 percent are probably taking up space in a landfill.

Ian Batey (United Arab Emirates) found another use for aluminum cans. He crushed them with a 20,000-pound monster truck! During the attempt, 82,800 aluminum cans were set up, but only 61,106 cans were crushed after three minutes.

1. List three reasons why recycling is important.

   1. _____

   2. _____

   3. _____

2. Could Batey's crushing of aluminum cans with a monster truck be considered recycling? Explain your answer.

   _____

   _____

3. Circle five words you read on page 34 to complete the word search. Use the word bank to help you.

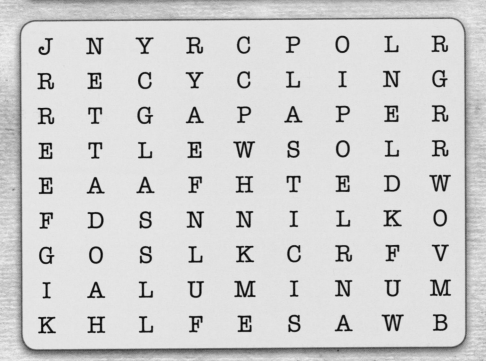

paper   glass   plastic   aluminum   recycling

```
J  N  Y  R  C  P  O  L  R
R  E  C  Y  C  L  I  N  G
R  T  G  A  P  A  P  E  R
E  T  L  E  W  S  O  L  R
E  A  A  F  H  T  E  D  W
F  D  S  N  N  I  L  K  O
G  O  S  L  K  C  R  F  V
I  A  L  U  M  I  N  U  M
K  H  L  F  E  S  A  W  B
```

4. How many aluminum cans are used in your house each week? If 60 percent of those cans are recycled, how many are not recycled?

   _____

Photo: Guinness World Records Limited

Kevin Fast (Canada) pulled a CC-177 Globemaster III aircraft weighing 416,299 lb. (188.83 metric tons) on September 17, 2009.

Did You Know?
Fast pulled the aircraft for a distance of 28 ft. 10.5 in. (8.8 m) in 1 minute 16 seconds.

ACTIVITIES

1. There are 2,000 pounds in one ton. How many tons did Fast pull?

   _____

2. Would it be easier to pull something with wheels or without wheels? Explain your answer.

   _____

3. Explain why Fast's first step was probably the most difficult.

   _____

Most Continuous Front Wheel Hops on a Bicycle

Photo: Guinness World Records Limited

Oliver Rege (Italy) performed 378 continuous front wheel hops on a bicycle in Turin, Italy, on April 8, 2011.

Did You Know?
The front tire was lifted off the ground repeatedly. No other part of the bicycle or the rider could touch the ground.

ACTIVITIES

1. If Rege did one bicycle hop every 2.5 seconds, how many seconds would it take him to do 378 hops?

   _____

2. How many minutes would it take him to do 378 jumps? (Hint: Use your answer to #1.)

   _____

3. How many times in a row can you hop?

   _____

Planet With the Most Moons

The planet Jupiter has 63 natural satellites. Most are small, irregularly shaped bodies of ice and rock.

Did You Know?
Saturn, with 61, has the second greatest number of moons.

Photo: Courtesy of NASA

ACTIVITIES

This sentence is a mnemonic device that can help you remember the order of the planets in our solar system: <u>M</u>y <u>v</u>ery <u>e</u>xcellent <u>m</u>other <u>j</u>ust <u>s</u>erved <u>u</u>s <u>n</u>oodles. Write the names of the planets in order, starting with the planet closest to the sun.

1. _____
2. _____
3. _____
4. _____
5. _____
6. _____
7. _____
8. _____

Most Times to Take Off and Land in One Hour

Photo: Guinness World Records Limited

Steve Slade (UK) performed 102 successive takeoffs and landings in a RANS S6 light aircraft in one hour on July 27, 2002.

Did You Know?
The plane did not stop between landings and takeoffs, but its wheels did touch down.

ACTIVITIES

1. How many takeoffs and landings did Slade complete each minute? Use a calculator to find out.

   _____

2. Carefully observe a bird taking off and landing. To find a bird to watch, go outside or search for a video. What did you notice about the way the bird's body moves?

   _____

   _____

Most Water-Skiers Towed Behind a Single Boat

Photo: Guinness World Records Limited

The most water-skiers towed behind a single boat is 114 by the Horsehead Water Ski Club (Australia) in Strahan, Tasmania, Australia, on March 28, 2010.

Did You Know?
Water-skiers travel at speeds up to 120 mph!

CHECK THIS OUT!

What is the first thing that comes to mind when you hear the word *skiing*? Do you picture being bundled up in a snowsuit, gliding down a snow-covered mountain? Or do you picture waterskiing instead?

Waterskiing is a sport where a person, wearing skis, is towed behind a boat. Some people do waterskiing tricks, like jumping or racing. Some people even water-ski barefoot!

In March 2010, a ski club in Australia set the record for the Most Water-Skiers Towed Behind a Single Boat with 114 people! The club had attempted the record on seven previous occasions over four years before they were finally successful. During this attempt, the skiers were towed a total of 1.29 miles.

1. Complete the crossword puzzle with words you read on page 40.

Across

4. A ski club in this country set the record for Most Water-Skiers Towed Behind a Single Boat.

6. You would need this to ski down a mountain.

Down

1. One type of waterskiing trick

2. Waterskiing is a _____ .

3. Some people water-ski _____ .

5. The club attempted to set the record _____ times before being successful.

2. How many people were involved in setting the record for Most Water-Skiers Towed Behind a Single Boat?

a. 28

b. 4

c. 7

d. 114

3. Have you ever been snow skiing or waterskiing? Which would you rather do? Explain your answer.

_____

_____

Most Concrete Blocks Broken in 30 Seconds

Photo: Guinness World Records Limited

Ali Bahçetepe (Turkey) used his hands to break 655 concrete blocks in 30 seconds on November 11, 2009.

Did You Know?

Bahçetepe set another record the same day for breaking 1,077 concrete blocks in one minute.

ACTIVITIES

1. In Bahçetepe's first record, about how many blocks were broken each second? Round to the nearest tenth.

_____

2. Have a contest with a friend. Who can draw the most stars, circles, or other shapes in 30 seconds? Write the winning record.

_____

Most People to Tandem Parachute in 24 Hours

Photo: Guinness World Records Limited

At a charity event in Lincolnshire, United Kingdom, 128 tandem parachute jumps were made in 24 hours on June 28, 2004.

Did You Know?

In tandem parachuting, a beginner is harnessed to an experienced skydiving instructor.

ACTIVITIES

Write the number 2 beside activities you would rather do in tandem with a friend or partner. Write 1 beside things you would choose to do alone.

_____ watch a movie   _____ skydive

_____ play basketball   _____ complete a school project

_____ do a craft   _____ jump on a trampoline

_____ take a hike   _____ read a book

_____ listen to music   _____ play a card game

Fastest Speed for a Motorcycle Ridden Blindfolded

Photo: Guinness World Records Limited

Billy Baxter (UK) reached a speed of 164.87 mph (265.33 km/h) while riding a motorcycle unsighted in Wiltshire, United Kingdom, in 2003.

Did You Know?
To set the record, Baxter used a three-way radio to talk with two riders behind him.

ACTIVITIES

1. Find out what the speed limit is on the street or road where you live. How many miles per hour over that limit did Baxter's motorcycle travel?

_____

2. Have a friend blindfold you, then try to do a simple task such as tying your shoes. What was most difficult about functioning without your sight?

_____

Shortest Time to Ski Down Mt. Everest

Photo: ©2001 Corbis Corporation

Ski instructor Davo Karnicar (Slovenia) skied from the summit of Mt. Everest to Base Camp in five hours on October 7, 2000.

Did You Know?

Though it took Karnicar only five hours to ski down the mountain, it took him a month of climbing and camping to reach the summit!

ACTIVITIES

1. Karnicar's journey took five hours. What have you spent five hours doing in the past week?

   _____

2. Close your eyes and imagine you are skiing down Mt. Everest. What might be most fun about your journey?

   _____

3. What might be most difficult about your journey?

   _____

Oldest Person to Fly in a Hot Air Balloon

Photo: Guinness World Records Limited

Emma Carrol (USA) was 109 years 70 days old on July 27, 2004, when she made an hour-long flight in a hot air balloon in Ottumwa, Iowa.

Did You Know?

A hot air balloon was the first flying object to be able to successfully carry humans. Look at airplanes, helicopters, and spaceships, and you'll see how far technology has come!

CHECK THIS OUT!

Emma Carrol (United States) was born on May 18, 1895, which made her 109 years old when she flew in a hot air balloon. Carrol lived for more than a century. A century is 100 years. A lot can happen in a century!

The first time a person flew in a hot air balloon was in 1783, over two centuries ago. A balloon carrying two men traveled over Paris, France, for 5.5 miles, staying in the air for 23 minutes.

Hot air balloons are still popular today, possibly because of their beauty. Hot air balloons come in many shapes and colors. Many cities around the United States host hot air balloon festivals throughout the year. These festivals can include balloon races, night glows (in which balloons are fired up while remaining tethered to the ground), and rides.

ACTIVITIES

1. If you owned a hot air balloon, what would it look like? Design it here.

2. Finish the sentence.

   A century is _____ years.

3. What does *tethered* mean?

   a. tied

   b. above

   c. parallel

   d. next

4. If the first hot air balloon traveled 5.5 miles in 23 minutes, about how many miles would it travel in one hour? Round your answer to the nearest whole number.

   _____

5. The first hot air balloon flight was in 1783. How many years ago was that? Circle your answer.

   more than two centuries   **less than two centuries**

6. Find Iowa on a map of the United States. What is its capital?

   _____

Longest Time Spent Living Underwater

Photo: ©2004 image100ltd

Richard Presley (USA) spent 69 days 19 minutes in a module underwater as part of Project Atlantis in Florida in 1992.

Did You Know?
The mission of Project Atlantis was to explore the human factors of living in an undersea environment.

ACTIVITIES

1. About how many weeks did Presley spend underwater?

_____

2. What do humans need that isn't found underwater? What would allow humans to survive underwater for a long time?

_____

_____

_____

Fastest Reverse Drive Over 500 Miles

Photo: ©2001 Brand X Pictures

Driving in reverse, Rob Gibney (Canada) covered 501.69 miles (807.39 km) at an average speed of 41.42 mph (66.67 km/h).

Did You Know?
Gibney set the record while driving on a racetrack in Calgary, Alberta, Canada.

ACTIVITIES

1. Gibney's speed averaged 41.42 miles per hour. Is that a slow, average, or fast speed for a car?

   _____

2. What factors do you think affected Gibney's speed?

   _____

3. Find a safe area and race with a friend. Race forward and then backward. Which race was faster?

   _____

Heaviest Vehicle Pulled With an Arm Wrestling Move

Photo: Guinness World Records Limited

Kevin Fast (Canada) pulled the heaviest vehicle using an arm wrestling move. He pulled a fire truck weighing 23,236 lb. (10,540 kg) in Cobourg, Ontario, Canada, on January 27, 2011.

Did You Know?

In order to qualify for the record, Fast needed to move the vehicle at least 12 in. (30 cm).

ACTIVITIES

1. The Heaviest Vehicle Pulled by Hair was a truck weighing 20,690 pounds. How much heavier was the fire truck that Fast pulled?

_____

2. Professional wrestlers use colorful stage names. What wrestling name would you choose?

_____

3. When you watch a professional wrestling match, do you think the fighting is real? Explain why or why not.

_____

Most Roller Coasters Ridden in 24 Hours

Photo: Guinness World Records Limited

Four friends (Philip A. Guarno, Adam Spivak, John R. Kirkwood, and Aaron Monroe Rye, all USA) rode 74 different roller coasters in 24 hours in 2001.

Did You Know?

The riders traveled by helicopter to visit 10 parks in four states.

ACTIVITIES

1. How many more coasters would bring the record to 100?

_____

2. About how many different roller coasters have you ridden?

_____

3. Would you rather ride your favorite roller coaster five times or ride five different coasters? Explain your answer.

_____

_____

Fastest Half Marathon Barefoot on Ice/Snow

Photo: Guinness World Records Limited

Wim Hof (Netherlands) ran the fastest half marathon while barefoot on ice or snow in 2 hours 16 minutes 34 seconds. He completed the half marathon near Oulu, Finland, on January 26, 2007.

Did You Know?

In November 2011, Hof also set the record for spending the longest time in direct, full-body contact with ice at 1 hour 52 minutes 42 seconds.

CHECK THIS OUT!

Brrr! Could you imagine running (or even standing!) on snow or ice ... with no shoes on? Not only did Wim Hof (Netherlands) do just that, but he set the world record for running the Fastest Half Marathon Barefoot on Ice or Snow. He completed 13.1 miles in just over two hours!

You may be wondering how this is even possible. Wouldn't his feet freeze? Well, Hof says he uses yoga techniques to regulate his body temperature and keep it at a normal 98.6°F, even in extreme cold. He is no stranger to extreme conditions, as he has been involved in various outdoor activities for over 20 years, including rock climbing, canyoning, waterfall climbing, and ice diving.

1. What is the normal human body temperature?

   a. 98.6°F

   b. 37°F

   c. 99°F

   d. 32°F

2. What is the freezing point for water in degrees Fahrenheit? Do some research if you need to. Circle your answer.

   more than 30°F   **less than 0°F**

3. What is your favorite thing to do in the winter? Draw a picture of it here.

4. How much longer did Hof spend running a half marathon barefoot than he spent in full-body contact with ice?

   _____

5. If a half marathon is 13.1 miles, how long is a full marathon?

   _____

Fastest Motorcycle Wheelie on a Tightrope

Photo: Guinness World Records Limited

Johann Traber (Germany) did a motorcycle wheelie on a tightrope at 32.9 mph (53 km/h) on August 13, 2005.

Did You Know?
An assistant sat on a solid trapeze below the tightrope to balance the motorcycle.

ACTIVITIES

1. The word part *cycle* means "circle" or "wheel." Write *cycle* to complete each word.

   bi _____   re _____

   uni _____   motor _____

   tri _____

2. Make a "tightrope" by laying a piece of string on the floor or making a line outside with sidewalk chalk. Walk, hop, and skip on the line without "falling." What was easiest? Most difficult?

_____

Lowest Temperature on Earth

Photo: Digital Vision®

A record low temperature of -128.6°F (-89.2°C) was registered at Vostok, Antarctica, on July 21, 1983.

Did You Know?
At the Vostok scientific station in Antarctica, scientists use ice core samples to study air trapped in the ice long ago.

ACTIVITIES

1. What is the lowest temperature on record for the city or state where you live? This Web site may help you: weather.gov.

_____

2. Use your answer to #1. How many degrees colder is the Lowest Temperature on Earth?

_____

3. Antarctica is the coldest, driest, windiest place on Earth. Would you like to visit there? Explain why or why not.

_____

Fastest Half Marathon Wearing a Gas Mask

Photo: Guinness World Records Limited

In New York City in 2010, Christopher Filipowski (USA) ran a half marathon wearing a functioning gas mask in 2 hours 36 minutes 59 seconds.

Did You Know?
Filipowski ran as his self-created character "The Swineflu Avenger."

ACTIVITIES

1. About how many minutes did it take Filipowski to complete the half marathon? Round to the nearest minute.

_____

2. A half marathon is about 13 miles long. Use your answer to #1 to find out what part of a mile Filipowski ran each minute. Round to the nearest hundredth.

_____

Fastest Whip

Photo: Guinness World Records Limited

Adam Winrich (USA) holds the world record for whip-cracking speed and accuracy. He hit 10 targets consecutively in 4.85 seconds in 2008.

Did You Know?
Winrich's stage name is "Adam Crack."

ACTIVITIES

1. To do something *accurately*, you must pay attention to detail so the job is complete and free from errors. What do you do with accuracy? Do you check math problems, throw balls, or play an instrument? Write one example.

   _____

2. Place 10 coins on a tabletop. How many seconds does it take you to grab and stack all the coins? Have a friend time you.

   _____

Fastest 100 Meter Light Aircraft Pull

Photo: Guinness World Records Limited

The fastest 100 m light aircraft pull was 29.84 seconds and was achieved by Montystar Agarawal (India) in Baramati, Maharashtra, India, on February 23, 2011.

Did You Know?
Chess was invented in India.

CHECK THIS OUT!

There are many types of competitions, such as dance competitions, band competitions, and cheerleading competitions, just to name a few. Some people push themselves to perform their very best during competitions with other people, in hopes of becoming the victor!

Two competitors—Montystar Agarawal and Mahendra Joshi, both Indian "strongmen"—pitted themselves against one another to see who could pull an aircraft 100 meters in the fastest time. Agarawal achieved the record, beating Joshi's time by only 0.82 seconds!

Before the competition began, it was ensured that both competitors had an equal advantage. Both aircraft weighed exactly the same because additional weight was added to the lighter aircraft.

ACTIVITIES

1. Why do you think it was verified that both aircraft weighed the same amount? What might happen if it had not been verified?

   _____

   _____

2. What does *victor* mean?

   a. fan

   b. lead

   c. winner

   d. loser

3. Have you participated in any competitions? What kind? Write a story about what happened during your competition.

   _____

   _____

   _____

   _____

4. Agarawal's time was 29.84 seconds. What was Joshi's time?

   a. 30.66 seconds

   b. 29.02 seconds

   c. 29.92 seconds

   d. 29.76 seconds

5. One meter equals 1.09 yards. How many feet did Agarawal pull the aircraft?

   _____

6. Agarawal beat Joshi's time by less than one second. True or false? Circle your answer.

   true   false

Largest Hiking Boot

Markus Appelman (Germany) made a boot that measures 23 ft. 5 in. (7.14 m) long, 8 ft. 2 in. (2.5 m) wide, and 13 ft. 9 in. (4.2 m) tall. It weighs 3,306.93 lb. (1,500 kg).

Photo: Guinness World Records Limited

Did You Know?

The shoelace for this hiking boot is 114 ft. 9 in. (35 m) long and would stretch as high as a giant Ferris wheel.

ACTIVITIES

1. How much would a pair of the largest hiking boots weigh?

   _____

2. Unscramble things you might see on a hike through the woods.

   reirqusl _____   **dowrilfewl** _____

   niep erte _____   **tesmar** _____

   kawh _____   **meowad** _____

Greatest Distance on Theme Park Rides in One Hour

Photo: Guinness World Records Limited

On September 14, 2003, Kerry-Ann Marshall (UK) traveled a total distance of 17,047 ft. (5,196 m) in 37 minutes on theme park rides at Thorpe Park, Chertsey, Surrey, United Kingdom.

Did You Know?
Thorpe Park is also home to the Colossus, a steel roller coaster that turns riders upside down 10 times!

ACTIVITIES

Why don't you fall out of your seat at the top of a loop on a roller coaster? Centrifugal force counteracts gravity and holds you in, even when you are upside down.

To see centrifugal force, do this experiment. Find a bucket with a handle and fill it $\frac{2}{3}$ full of water. Go outside. Now swing the bucket by its handle in a wide loop, over and over. Describe what happens to the water.

_____

_____

_____

Tallest Rideable Motorcycle

Photo: Guinness World Records Limited

In 2005, Gregory Dunham (USA) built a motorcycle that is 20 ft. 4 in. (6.187 m) long and 11 ft. 3 in. (3.429 m) tall.

Did You Know?

The motorcycle weighs 6,500 lb. and is powered by an 8.2 L V8 engine. The tires are 74 in. tall.

ACTIVITIES

1. How many inches would the Tallest Rideable Motorcycle's tires reach over your head?

   _____

2. Two thousand pounds equals one ton. How many tons does the motorcycle weigh? Use a fraction in your answer.

   _____

3. Where would you go on the world's Tallest Rideable Motorcycle?

   _____

Fastest Jet-Powered Model Aircraft (Remote-Controlled)

Photo: Guinness World Records Limited

A remote-controlled, jet-powered model aircraft created by Axel Haché (Dominican Republic) and David Shulman (USA) reached a speed of 293 Knots, or 337.18 mph (542.64 km/h) in 2010.

Did You Know?

The AMA (Academy of Model Aeronautics) certifies model plane flying records in the United States.

ACTIVITIES

1. Commercial jets fly at about 500 miles per hour. How many mph faster would the model jet need to be to reach this speed?

   _____

2. Knots measure the speed of ships and planes. A Knot equals 6,076 feet per hour. How many feet per hour is three Knots?

   _____

3. Look at a map. What is the capital of the Caribbean nation the Dominican Republic?

   _____

Fastest 100-Meter Bike Sled Race on Sand With Four Dogs

Photo: Guinness World Records Limited

Four dogs pulled Suzannah Sorrell (UK) 100 m in 11.65 seconds. The sprint took place in Holkham, Norfolk, United Kingdom, on November 6, 2007.

Did You Know?
Joe Redington is known as the "Father of the Iditarod." He raced in this famous dogsled race when he was 80 years old!

ACTIVITIES

1. Llamas help carry loads on steep climbs. Dolphins have been trained to locate underwater mines. Write three more ways animals help people.

_____

_____

_____

2. The Iditarod race ends each year in Nome, Alaska. Look at a map. Nome is on the coast of what body of water?

_____

Photo: Guinness World Records Limited

DARING SPORTS

Photo: Guinness World Records Limited

Fastest 50-Meter Altitude Descent by Canoe

Photo: Guinness World Records Limited

On November 4, 1994, Shaun Baker (UK) dropped 164 ft. (50 m) down a river in a canoe in 4 minutes 53 seconds in Snowdonia, Wales, United Kingdom.

Did You Know?
A four-person sprint kayak can reach speeds great enough to pull a water-skier.

ACTIVITIES

1. Niagara Falls is 168 feet tall. Did the record-breaking canoe fall more or less than the height of Niagara Falls? Circle your answer.

    more   **less**

2. The wind powers sailboats. Gasoline engines power motorboats. Human work powers canoes and rowboats. Which type of boat would you like to pilot? Explain your answer.

_____

_____

Longest Distance Cycled in One Hour With No Hands

Photo: Guinness World Records Limited

On June 23, 2009, Erik Skramstad (USA) cycled 23.25 mi. (37.417 km) without using his hands at the Las Vegas Motor Speedway in Las Vegas, Nevada.

Did You Know?

The fastest speed reached by a bicycle was 167 mph (269 km/h). The bicycle was ridden behind a windshield fitted to a dragster car.

ACTIVITIES

1. What place is about 23 miles from your home? Use a map or ask an adult for help.

_____

2. Circle things you can do without using your hands.

turn on a light   open a book

get under a blanket   open the refrigerator

knock on a door   catch a ball

Furthest Distance Skipping on a Rolling Globe

Photo: Guinness World Records Limited

Katya Davidson (USA) traveled 2,008 ft. 4 in. (612.13 m) while skipping on a rolling globe that was 24 in. (60 cm) tall. She accomplished this feat at the Red, White, and Blue Parade in Citrus Heights, California, on June 28, 2003.

Did You Know?

There are colleges where you can earn a degree in circus variety arts, such as acrobatics, gymnastics, juggling, and clowning.

ACTIVITIES

1. Davidson set her record during a parade. What could you do in a parade to entertain the crowd?

   _____

2. There are 5,280 feet in a mile. Did Davidson travel more or less than $\frac{1}{2}$ mile? Circle your answer.

   less than $\frac{1}{2}$ mile   **more than $\frac{1}{2}$ mile**

3. How many times can you skip rope without stopping?

   _____

Largest Snow Softball Tournament

Photo: Guinness World Records Limited

In Barre, Vermont, 795 players on 61 teams participated in the Freezing Fun For Families Winter Coed Softball Tournament from March 6-8, 2009.

Did You Know?

This tournament raises money for Vermont families who have children with life-threatening illnesses.

ACTIVITIES

1. About how many people were on each team in the snow tournament? Round to the nearest whole number.

   _____

2. Many popular expressions come from baseball and softball. If someone looks at your test grade and says you "hit a homerun," what do they mean?

   _____

   _____

Most Basketballs Spun Simultaneously on a Frame

Photo: Guinness World Records Limited

On May 25, 1999, Michael Kettman (USA) spun 28 regulation-sized basketballs simultaneously for five seconds.

Did You Know?

YMCA teacher James A. Naismith invented basketball in 1891. The first games were played by landing the ball in peach baskets at each end of a gym.

CHECK THIS OUT!

Can you spin a basketball on your finger? Michael Kettman (United States) probably can! In 1999, he broke the world record for the Most Basketballs Spun Simultaneously on a Frame.

Kettman began spinning basketballs when he was four years old. In 1987, when he was 15, he set a goal of spinning the most basketballs. The record at the time was eight balls. He practiced six to eight hours every day for 21 days, and then was able to break the record by spinning 10 balls. That record was broken a few years later.

In 1997, Kettman decided to regain the record. For his next attempt, he kept 20 balls spinning at the same time! But he didn't stop there. His record now stands at 28!

ACTIVITIES

1. Finish the sentence.

   A standard basketball weighs 22 ounces. Kettman was spinning a total

   of _____ pounds, _____ ounces when he broke the current record.

2. Make a time line of Kettman's life starting at the year he was born and including dates from the passage on page 70.

   1972

3. If Kettman practiced an average of seven hours a day for 21 days, how many total hours did he practice to break his first record?

   a. 126

   b. 21

   c. 168

   d. 147

4. Kettman originally set the world record by spinning eight balls. True or false? Circle your answer.

   true   false

5. Set a goal for yourself. How many hours a day will you practice to achieve your goal? Give yourself a week of practice, then come back and write about your progress toward accomplishing your goal.

   _____

   _____

   _____

Largest Returning Boomerang

Photo: Guinness World Records Limited

On July 1, 2008, Gerhard Walter (Austria) threw an 8 ft. 5 in. (2.57 m) boomerang at the University Sports Centre in Graz, Austria.

Did You Know?
The oldest known boomerang is 20,000 years old and was discovered in Poland.

ACTIVITIES

1. How many more inches would be needed for a nine-foot boomerang?

_____

2. The word *boomerang* contains *oo*. Write *oo* to complete each word.

ahch ____ ____   sch ____ ____ l

d ____ ____ dle   h ____ ____ ray

bab ____ ____ n   r ____ ____ ster

ball ____ ____ n   z ____ ____ m

Longest Jump on a Unicycle

Photo: Guinness World Records Limited

David Weichenberger (Austria) jumped a unicycle 9 ft. 8 in. (2.95 m) during the Vienna Recordia, in Vienna, Austria, on September 16, 2006.

Did You Know?

On January 29, 2004, Sem Abrahams (USA) rode a 114 ft. 10 in. (35 m) tall unicycle for 27 ft. 10 in. (8.5 m).

ACTIVITIES

1. The record was set in 2006. How many years ago was that?

   _____

2. Most ceilings are eight feet tall. Did the unicyclist jump higher than most ceilings? Circle your answer.

   yes   **no**

3. A unicycle has one wheel. A bicycle has two. What do you call a bike with three wheels?

Largest Soccer Shirt

Photo: Guinness World Records Limited

On April 5, 2009, a soccer shirt measuring 234 ft. 1 in. by 259 ft. 8 in. (71.35 m by 79.15 m) was presented in Sukru San, Istanbul, Turkey.

Did You Know?
Soccer players exchange jerseys at the end of a game as a sign of respect and good sportsmanship.

ACTIVITIES

1. What would be a good name for a team of giant soccer players wearing giant shirts?

   _____

2. In soccer, a defender kicks the ball away from the opposing team. A striker tries to shoot the ball into the goal. The goalie defends the goal. Which position would be best for you? Explain your answer.

   _____

   _____

Greatest Distance on Inline Skates in 24 Hours (Men)

Photo: Guinness World Records Limited

For two days in June 2004, Mauro Guenci (Italy) covered 337.8 mi. (543.6 km) on inline skates on a measured street circuit in Senigallia, Italy.

Did You Know?

Russell "Rusty" Moncrief crossed the United States on inline skates in only 69 days.

ACTIVITIES

1. The record holder skated about 337 miles. Have you been on a trip more than 300 miles away from home? Where did you go or where would you like to go?

   _____

2. Circle your favorite ways to travel on wheels.

   roller skates   **skateboard**

   bicycle   **scooter**

Fastest Marathon on Stilts

Photo: Guinness World Records Limited

Michelle Frost (UK) completed the Flora London Marathon on stilts in 8 hours 25 minutes on April 13, 2008, in London, United Kingdom.

CHECK THIS OUT!

Over 35,000 runners participated in the marathon, but Michelle Frost (United Kingdom) was the tallest. No other runner was even close! That's because Frost ran on four-foot stilts!

Frost had learned to walk on stilts eight years earlier. She wanted to raise money for charity, and thought that running a marathon on stilts might help. To prepare for the race, she trained hard. She fell several times, but fortunately, she trained on grass. In the marathon, she ran on paved streets, so any fall during the race would have really hurt. Somehow, she made it without falling.

As she hoped, her race drew lots of attention. Frost raised over $10,000 for charity!

ACTIVITIES

1. Frost took several bad falls during the marathon. True or false? Circle your answer.

                      true   **false**

2. What does *participated* mean? What was the last time you participated in something?

   _____

   _____

3. Why do you think Frost trained on grass instead of pavement?

   _____

   _____

4. How much money did Frost raise for charity?

   a. $35,000

   b. $10,000

   c. $1.2 million

   d. $1.5 million

5. Imagine that you want to raise money for your favorite charity. You might not be able to run a marathon on stilts, but think of some activity you could do to help. Design a flyer asking people to support you by donating money to your charity. Draw it here.

Longest Tightrope Crossing by Bicycle

Photo: Guinness World Records Limited

On October 15, 2008, Nik Wallenda (USA) crossed a tightrope on a bicycle in Newark, New Jersey. The 235 ft. (71.63 m) tightrope was suspended 135 ft. (41.15 m) in the air.

Did You Know?

Daredevil Charles Blondin crossed Niagara Falls on a tightrope while wearing stilts; wearing a blindfold; pushing a wheelbarrow; and carrying his manager.

ACTIVITIES

1. What's the highest place you have ever been?

_____

2. A *phobia* is a fear. Fear of heights is called *acrophobia*. *Claustrophobia* is a fear of tight spaces. *Arachnophobia* is the fear of spiders. Write one of your fears.

_____

3. What jobs require workers to be high off the ground?

_____

Furthest Distance on a Snowmobile on Water

On September 3, 2005, Kyle Nelson (Canada) rode a snowmobile for 43.3 mi. (69.68 km) on Cowan Lake, Canada.

Did You Know?

In the United States, there are about 1.65 million registered snowmobiles. In Canada, there are about 765,275 registered snowmobiles.

Photo: Guinness World Records Limited

ACTIVITIES

1. How many more miles would Nelson need to ride for a 75-mile record?

_____

2. A seaplane travels in the air and on water. An amphibious vehicle works on land and in water. What kind of multi-terrain vehicle would you like to invent? Draw it below.

Largest Dance Class (Multi-Venue)

Photo: Guinness World Records Limited

On July 11, 2008, students across Liverpool, United Kingdom, participated in a multiple-venue dance class. There were 26,797 primary school students involved in the event.

Did You Know?
Birds are the only animals that can dance in rhythm to music.

ACTIVITIES

1. If you were in charge of a party for thousands of kids your age, what fun activity would you plan for everyone to do?

_____

2. Circle dances you like to do.

Chicken Dance	Hokey-Pokey
Limbo Dance	YMCA
Cha Cha Slide	Locomotion

Oldest Tandem Parachute Jump (Female)

Photo: Guinness World Records Limited

On September 30, 2004, Estrid Geersten (Denmark) made a tandem parachute jump at the age of 100 years 60 days. She jumped from an altitude of 13,123 ft. (4,000 m) over Roskilde, Denmark.

Did You Know?

Mike Forsythe (USA) and his dog, Cara, parachuted from an aircraft at a record altitude of 30,100 ft. (9,174 m), the highest parachute jump by a man/dog team.

ACTIVITIES

1. What year will it be when you are 100 years old?

   _____

2. Some people make lists of things they want to do in their lifetimes. They include places to visit and things to try. Write three things you would like to do someday.

   _____

   _____

   _____

Largest Egg and Spoon Race

Photo: Guinness World Records Limited

The largest egg and spoon race was achieved by 1,308 students at Singapore Polytechnic, Singapore, on July 27, 2008.

Did You Know?

You can tell if an egg is raw or boiled by spinning it. Raw eggs wobble and cooked eggs spin.

CHECK THIS OUT!

Ready, set, go!

It was July 27, 2008, and 1,308 people stood at the starting line. They had gathered to run in the world's Largest Egg and Spoon Race. It sounds easy, but it is hard to balance a two-ounce raw egg in a spoon while running. The egg rolls as the runner takes each step, and many eggs fall off. How many crossed the finish line with the egg still in the spoon? The judges did not count the finishers because that was not important to the record. They just counted the people who started!

On March 13, 2009, another quirky race took place. Five hundred thirty-nine people ran a race in Belgium backward! They set the record for the Largest Backward Race.

ACTIVITIES

1. Draw a line of symmetry on the egg below.

2. Finish the sentence.

The record-setting egg and spoon race needed _____ dozen eggs.

3. If 825 people completed the egg and spoon race, how many racers dropped their eggs?

_____

4. Which race had more participants, the egg and spoon race or the backward race? Circle your answer.

egg and spoon race   **backward race**

5. Write <, >, or = to complete the equation.

1,308 539

6. Go outside and practice walking with an egg balanced on a spoon. How far can you walk before the egg drops?

_____

_____

Highest Shallow Dive

Darren Taylor (USA) dove into 11.8 inches (30 cm) of water from a height of 36 ft. 5.4 in. (11.11 m) in London, United Kingdom, on June 12, 2011.

Photo: Guinness World Records Limited

Did You Know?
Taylor holds many records for shallow diving. His nickname is "Professor Splash."

ACTIVITIES

1. For Taylor's dive, was the water more or less than one foot deep? Circle your answer.

   less than one foot   **more than one foot**

2. Diving is safe only in very deep water. Circle the swimming pool depth you like best for swimming and playing in the water.

   2-foot: shallow zone   **4-foot:** medium-depth zone

   6-foot: deep zone   **15-foot:** diving zone

Most Backflips on a Kick Scooter (Single Jump)

Photo: Guinness World Records Limited

Jarret Reid (USA) of Anaheim, California, completed a single scooter backflip, landing with both feet on the scooter at Van Nuys Airport, California, on January 21, 2001.

Did You Know?

In 2000, more than three million Razor® scooters were sold in the United States. Each scooter cost about $100.

ACTIVITIES

1. If a $125 scooter were on sale for one-half off, how much would it cost?

_____

2. Invent a new feature or accessory that kids would love to have for their scooters. Draw it on this scooter.

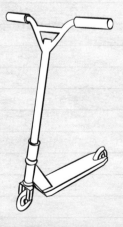

Greatest Distance by Pedal-Powered Boat in 24 Hours (Team)

Photo: Guinness World Records Limited

On May 7, 2005, the Trieste Waterbike Team (Italy) covered a distance of 110.2 mi. (177.3 km) in a pedal-powered boat in 24 hours in Trieste, Italy.

Did You Know?
Jason Lewis and Lourdes Arango crossed 450 nautical mi. (833.4 km) of the Timor Sea in 11 days in a 26-ft. (7.9-m) pedal-powered boat.

ACTIVITIES

1. What would you like to power by pedaling?

_____

2. How many more miles would the pedal-powered boat have to travel to reach 250 miles?

_____

3. Make a boat from recycled materials you find, such as clean foam pieces and old containers. Write what you did.

_____

Highest Wall Ride on a Skateboard

Photo: Guinness World Records Limited

Brad Edwards and Aaron Murray (both USA) rode 7 ft. 6 in. (2.29 m) up a wall on their skateboards at the Hollywood Skate Jam in Hollywood, California, on August 25, 2006.

Did You Know?

Skateboarding first became an extreme sport in 1995 as part of ESPN's *X Games*.

ACTIVITIES

1. Geckos can climb walls easily using millions of tiny hairs, called *setae*, on the bottom of their feet. Where would you climb if you were a gecko?

   _____

2. How many inches did the skateboarders ride up the wall?

   _____

3. Give one rule you know for skateboarding safely.

   _____

Deepest Cycling Under Water

Photo: Guinness World Records Limited

Vittorio Innocente (Italy) cycled at a depth of 214 ft. 10 in. (66.5 m) under water in Santa Margherita Ligure, Italy, on July 21, 2008.

Did You Know?

Water spiders trap air bubbles with their hairy legs and abdomens, then store them in "scuba tanks" spun of their own silk.

CHECK THIS OUT!

Vittorio Innocente (Italy) broke the world record for the Deepest Cycling Under Water. He smashed his own record set three years earlier. This time, he went down 214 feet, 10 inches. That is like going down 20 sets of stairs!

How did he do it? First, he put on scuba diving gear to help him breathe underwater. With help from other scuba divers, he was able to descend to the ocean floor. At 92 feet, the ocean floor sloped away and went even deeper. Innocente got on his mountain bike and began pedaling. He had to be careful of mud pools and large rocks in his path.

Innocente made his wild ride for two reasons. He wanted to raise money for charity. Also, he wanted to prove that mountain bikes can go anywhere, maybe even the surface of the moon!

ACTIVITIES

1. An *antonym* is a word that has the opposite meaning of another word. Which is an antonym of *descend*?

   a. shout

   b. start

   c. ascend

   d. increase

2. What are two reasons why Innocente made his wild ride?

   1. _____

   2. _____

3. Whose record did Innocente break?

   _____

4. Describe the challenges that Innocente faced as he rode down the underwater slope.

   _____

   _____

5. People should not go in the ocean and disturb the creatures there just to set a record. Do you agree or disagree with this statement? Explain your answer.

   _____

   _____

   _____

6. Unscramble words you read on page 88.

   inycglc   _____

   tdunrerwae   _____

   nuonmita kbei   _____

Fastest 10K Race in a Costume (Two Person)

Photo: Guinness World Records Limited

On December 3, 2006, Stuart Maycock and Shaun Marsden (both UK) completed the Percy Pud 10K road race in a two-person costume in 40 minutes 18 seconds. The race took place in Loxley, Sheffield, South Yorkshire, United Kingdom.

Did You Know?

Running barefoot may be better for your feet than running with traditional jogging shoes.

ACTIVITIES

Think about your favorite cartoon characters, sports mascots, and superheroes. If they raced each other, who would win? Write the names of four characters who might race and tell who you think will win.

Runners

_____

_____

_____

_____

Winner

Largest Sneaker

Photo: Guinness World Records Limited

A sneaker measuring 13 ft. 1 in. (4 m) long, 5 ft. 3 in. (1.6 m) wide, and 5 ft. 7 in. (1.7 m) high was made on behalf of the UK's Race for Life. It was created in Cardiff, United Kingdom, in March 2009.

Did You Know?

The plastic tip at the end of a shoelace is called an *aglet*. If it wasn't there, we wouldn't be able to thread our shoelaces through the eyelets of our shoes.

ACTIVITIES

1. How many more inches would make the Largest Sneaker six feet high?

   _____

2. Is the Largest Sneaker longer or shorter than the room you are standing in right now? Circle your answer.

   shorter   **longer**

3. What could a giant do while wearing giant sneakers?

   _____

Longest Ramp Jump on a Snowmobile

Photo: Guinness World Records Limited

On March 10, 2007, Ross Mercer (Canada) jumped a snowmobile 263 ft. 6 in. (80.31 m) in Steamboat Springs, Colorado.

Did You Know?
Mercer had to complete 66 jumps before the jump that broke the Guinness World Record.

ACTIVITIES

1. The number 263 is a *prime number*. A prime number can be divided evenly only by itself and the number one. Write three more prime numbers.

_____   _____   _____

2. The word *mobile* means "capable of moving." A snowmobile is capable of moving in the snow. The word part *auto* can mean "on its own." Define *automobile*.

_____

_____

Most Soccer Balls Juggled

Photo: Guinness World Records Limited

Victor Rubilar (Argentina) juggled five regulation-sized soccer balls for 10 seconds at the Gallerian Shopping Centre, Stockholm, Sweden, on November 4, 2006.

Did You Know?

A regular soccer ball has 32 leather panels—20 hexagons and 12 pentagons.

ACTIVITIES

1. Which would be easier to juggle—scarves or soccer balls? Explain your answer.

_____

_____

2. How many times can you throw and catch a ball in 10 seconds?

_____

3. On what continent can you find Argentina?

_____

Fastest Baseball Pitch (Female)

Photo: Guinness World Records Limited

On April 19, 2008, 15-year-old Lauren Boden (USA) pitched a baseball 65 mph (104.6 km/h).

Did You Know?

In 1875, a women's baseball club sprang up in Springfield, Illinois, that had two teams—the Blondes and the Brunettes.

CHECK THIS OUT!

Next time you are up at bat, be glad Lauren Boden (United States) is not the pitcher. She set the Guinness World Record for the world's Fastest Baseball Pitch by a Female. Her record pitch traveled 65 miles per hour!

Boden set this record on April 19, 2008, when she was only 15 years old. She also made history at her high school. She was the first girl to make the baseball team. Boden is one of a set of triplets. All three of the girls, plus a younger sister, play baseball.

Throwing a baseball isn't the same as throwing a softball. That record belongs to someone else. The record for the world's Fastest Softball Pitch by a Female is 68.9 miles per hour. Zara Mee (Australia) threw this pitch on May 8, 2005.

ACTIVITIES

1. Which is closest to the speed of Boden's baseball pitch?

   a. a child skating

   b. a car traveling through a parking lot

   c. a car traveling on a highway

   d. a dog running in a park

2. How did Boden make history at her high school?

   _____

3. How much faster did the Fastest Softball Pitch travel than Boden's baseball?

   a. 3.9 mph

   b. 4.9 mph

   c. 68.9 mph

   d. 65 mph

4. Round the speed of Mee's pitch to the nearest whole number.

   _____

5. Boden is one of a set of twins. True or false? Circle your answer.

   true   **false**

6. Play a game of catch with a friend. How many times can the two of you catch the ball without dropping it?

   _____

Longest Somersault on Spring-Loaded Stilts

Photo: Guinness World Records Limited

John Simkins (UK) somersaulted 16 ft. 6 in. (5.04 m) on power stilts on June 18, 2009, on the set of *Zheng Da Zong Yi - Guinness World Records Special* in Beijing, China.

Did You Know?
While wearing spring-loaded stilts, you can jump 6 ft. (1.8 m) in the air, run 25 mph (10.23 km/h), and take 9 ft. (2.7 m) long strides.

ACTIVITIES

1. Write what you would do if you had spring-loaded stilts.

_____

2. How far could you travel in eight strides wearing spring-loaded stilts?

_____

3. How many somersaults can you do in a row?

_____

Most Women's Log Rolling World Championships

Photo: Guinness World Records Limited

Tina Bosworth (USA) won the World Lumberjack Championships in 1990, 1992, 1996, 1997, 1998, 1999, 2000, 2001, and 2002.

Did You Know?

In 1894, a seven-mile-long log jam clogged the Mississippi River and took six months to clear. It was estimated the log jam had over four billion feet of lumber.

ACTIVITIES

1. Circle lumberjack competition events you would like to try.

   log sawing   **tree chopping**

   log rolling   **tree climbing**

2. Have you read a tall tale about Paul Bunyan, the giant lumberjack? When he was born, he was so big that his parents had to use a lumber wagon as a baby carriage. Write another "fact" about Paul Bunyan.

_____

Most People Controlling Volleyballs

Photo: Guinness World Records Limited

On October 2, 2008, a group of people controlled 299 volleyballs at the YungShin Sports Park in Taichung County, Taiwan.

Did You Know?

William G. Morgan invented volleyball in 1895. He originally named it *mintonette*.

ACTIVITIES

1. How many more people would be needed to make it 500 people controlling volleyballs?

    _____

2. Volleyball players can serve the ball, set it, bump it, and spike it. Write one way you know how to hit a volleyball.

    _____

3. Few English words begin with *ll*. What word begins with *ll* and means "a long-necked animal related to the camel"?

    _____

Most Wins of the Mountain Bike World Championships (Four-Cross, Male)

Photo: Guinness World Records Limited

Brian Lopes (USA) took three four-cross mountain-biking world championship titles in 2002, 2005, and 2007.

Did You Know?
It is not uncommon for a downhill skateboarder to reach speeds over 50 mph (80.5 km/h).

ACTIVITIES

1. Would you rather bike on a mountain, on a paved bike path, or around your neighborhood? Explain your answer.

   _____

2. Lopes won in 2007. How many years ago was that?

   _____

3. Describe your bike or a bike you would like to have. Write what color and type it is and how many gears it has.

   _____

First Landed Wheelchair Backflip

Photo: Guinness World Records Limited

Aaron Fotheringham (USA) successfully landed a backflip with his wheelchair on October 25, 2008, in Las Vegas, Nevada.

Did You Know?

The Paralympic Games are for athletes with disabilities. Participants compete in nine sports such as skiing, shooting, swimming, and powerlifting.

CHECK THIS OUT!

Here comes Aaron Fotheringham (United States)! He is using his wheelchair as a skateboard!

Fotheringham is a special kind of athlete. He cannot walk, but that has never slowed him down. His interest in skateboarding began when he was a young boy. His brother thought that Fotheringham should skateboard in his wheelchair. Fotheringham practiced hard to learn to use his wheelchair. At age eight, he was able to perform tricks with it. Fotheringham was 14 years old when he set the record for the First Landed Wheelchair Backflip.

Fotheringham's nickname is "Wheels." People like to watch him in competition. Yet Fotheringham's greatest pride is working with children just like him. He shows them what they can do in a wheelchair.

1. What is an *athlete*? Why is Fotheringham a special kind of athlete?

   _____

   _____

2. Read the following statements. Circle *true* or *false*.

   Fotheringham was eight years old when he set his world record.

             true   **false**

   Fotheringham's nickname is "Flip."

             true   **false**

   Fotheringham performed his backflip in Los Angeles, California.

             true   **false**

3. What is Fotheringham's greatest pride?

   a. his work with children

   b. his world record

   c. his spins and jumps

   d. his athleticism

4. Fotheringham is a hero to both children and adults. Do you agree or disagree with this statement? Explain your answer.

   _____

5. Write about a time when you overcame a difficulty in order to accomplish something that made you proud.

   _____

   _____

6. Finish the sentence.

   Fotheringham is able to use his wheelchair like a skateboard

   because _____ .

Longest Kite Surfing Journey
(Female)

Photo: Guinness World Records Limited

Andreya Wharry (UK) kite surfed between Watergate Bay, Cornwall, United Kingdom, and Dungarven, Ireland, on September 7, 2005. The journey was 115.4 nautical mi. (213.72 km).

Did You Know?
When the winds are good, a kite surfer can race across the water at 40 mph (64.37 km/h) and complete jumps that are 30 feet (9.14 m) high.

ACTIVITIES

1. In kite surfing, the wind fills the kite and propels a board across the water. What else is powered by the wind?

   _____   _____

   _____   _____

2. A nautical mile is based on the circumference of Earth. The equator is an imaginary line like a belt around the middle of the planet. It divides Earth into two halves, or hemispheres. Which hemisphere do you live on?

   _____

Largest Soccer Ball

Photo: Guinness World Records Limited

The largest soccer ball measured 51 ft. 4 in. (15.66 m) in diameter. It was created in Johannesburg, South Africa, on July 5, 2010.

Did You Know?

The ball weighed 1,433 lb. (650 kg) and took 3.5 hours to inflate. It was tethered to the ground with 20 ropes to keep it from rolling away.

ACTIVITIES

1. The *diameter* is a line that passes through the center of a circle. Measure the diameter of this circle in inches.

   Diameter = _____

2. The FIFA World Cup is a soccer competition held every four years. It is the world's most popular sporting event. Write what country you will cheer for in the next World Cup.

_____

Most Sacrifice Bunts in a Baseball Career

Photo: Guinness World Records Limited

During his 20-year professional baseball career, between 1984 and 2003, Masahiro Kawai (Japan) made 514 sacrifice bunts.

Did You Know?
Little League Baseball and Softball is the world's largest organized youth sports program. It has approximately 2.6 million players.

ACTIVITIES

1. When a batter makes a sacrifice bunt, he or she helps the runner on base and gives up the chance for a big hit. What have you done to help a team or group?

_____

_____

2. About how many sacrifice bunts did Kawai make during each year of his career? Use a calculator to find out. Round to the nearest whole number.

_____

Most Items Kicked Off People's Heads in One Minute

Photo: Guinness World Records Limited

On the set of *Guinness World Records Smashed* at Pinewood Studios, United Kingdom, Zara Phythian (UK) kicked 43 items off of people's heads in one minute on March 25, 2009.

Did You Know?

Phythian kicked chocolate American footballs off of the helmets of the Hertfordshire Hurricanes.

ACTIVITIES

1. How high can you kick? Stretch your arm straight out. Can you kick and touch your fingertips with your toes? Circle your answer.

   yes   **no**

2. How many items could Phythian kick in 11 minutes?

   _____

3. Which would be easier to kick: something larger (like a football) or something smaller (like a tennis ball)? Explain your answer.

   _____

Fastest 100 Meters on a Space Hopper (Female)

Photo: Guinness World Records Limited

On September 6, 2004, in Fife, United Kingdom, Dee McDougall (UK) completed a 100-meter race on a space hopper in 39.88 seconds.

Did You Know?

The original space hopper landed in stores in 1971. Since then, it has been called a *moon hopper, hoppity hop, kangaroo ball, skippy ball,* or *hop ball.*

CHECK THIS OUT!

Dee McDougall (United Kingdom) covered 100 meters in a record 39.88 seconds. You might ask, "Why is that a big deal?" After all, top runners can do it in about 11 seconds. What made McDougall's time so noteworthy? The answer is that she did it while sitting on a giant rubber ball!

The ball that she used is called a *space hopper* in the United Kingdom, but it is known around the world by other names. It is basically a huge rubber ball with handles. It could be the size of a small beach ball or a very large one.

The goal is to sit on top of the ball and hop around. All you need to do is grab the handles. Then, begin to bounce. These balls are pretty safe toys, as they do not break easily. In fact, they are so strong that they can support 600 pounds!

ACTIVITIES

1. What is not another name for space hoppers?

    a. moon hopper

    b. hip hip hop

    c. kangaroo ball

    d. skippy ball

2. Finish the sentence.

    Space hoppers are made of _____ **.**

3. What does *noteworthy* mean? What is something noteworthy that has happened recently in your school or neighborhood?

    _____

    _____

4. How much do you weigh? If a space hopper can support 600 pounds, how many people your size could fit on one? Circle your answer.

    five or more   **less than five**

5. Circle the animals that can hop.

    grasshopper   **kangaroo**

    elephant   **rabbit**

    zebra   **koala**

6. What name for a space hopper do you think makes the most sense? Explain your answer. What name would you give to a space hopper?

    _____

    _____

    _____

Longest Rideable Surfboard

Photo: Guinness World Records Limited

On June 12, 2009, Rico De Souza (Brazil) rode a 30 ft. 10 in. (9.4 m) surfboard at Solemar Beach, Espirito Santo, Brazil.

Did You Know?
The earliest written account of surfing was made in 1779 by Lt. James King, while visiting Hawaii.

ACTIVITIES

1. A basketball hoop rises 10 feet off the ground. If you stood the Longest Rideable Surfboard on end, about how many basketball hoops tall would it be?

_____

2. Look at a map. What ocean is off the coast of Brazil?

_____

3. What water activity do you think is most fun?

_____

Furthest Distance by a Hand-Cranked Cycle in 24 Hours (Male)

Photo: Guinness World Records Limited

For two days in February 2009, Thomas Lange (Germany) used a hand-cranked cycle to cover a distance of 403.8 mi. (649.85 km) during the Bike Sebring 12/24 Hours in Sebring, Florida.

Did You Know?

Mike Augspurger invented the hand-cranked bicycle so people with disabilities could also enjoy cycling.

ACTIVITIES

1. Describe an invention that could help children with disabilities use the playground at your school.

   _____

   _____

2. Lange cycled for about 403 miles in 24 hours. About how many miles did he travel per hour? Use a calculator to find out.

   _____

Fastest 4 x 100-Meter Sack Relay Race

Photo: Guinness World Records Limited

On June 17, 2003, Andrew Rodaughan, Luke MacFarlane, Patrick Holcolmbe, and James Osbourne (all Australia) completed a 4 x 100-meter sack relay race at Ivanhoe Grammar School, Mernda, Victoria, Australia, in 2 minutes 29.09 seconds.

Did You Know?

In the United States, the average person eats 124 lb. (56.25 kg) of potatoes each year. The average person in Germany eats more than 200 lb. (90.72 kg) each year.

ACTIVITIES

There are about 109 yards in a 100-meter race. Set up a 100-meter race outside for you and your friends. Run the race in silly ways. Ask an adult to time you. Record your results in the chart.

Runners	Running	Sack Race (use old pillowcases)	Hopping on One Foot	Holding Cotton Ball on Spoon
1.	Time:	Time:	Time:	Time:
2.				
3.				
4.				

Most Wins of the IGSA Women's Downhill Skateboard Championships

Photo: Guinness World Records Limited

Angelina Nobre (Switzerland, 2004-2005), Jolanda Vogler (Switzerland, 2006-2007), and Brianne Davies (Canada, 2008-2009) have all won two IGSA (International Gravity Sports Association) Women's Downhill Skateboard Championships.

Did You Know?

In 2003, Ryan Sheckler became a pro skateboarder at the age of 13. That year, he had victories at the X Games, the Gravity Games, the Vans Triple Crown, and the Slam City Jam.

ACTIVITIES

1. Why do you think downhill skateboarding is called a *gravity sport*?

_____

2. Circle your favorite ways to travel downhill.

biking	skiing
skateboarding	rolling
snowboarding	somersaulting
sledding	water sliding

Largest Trick Roping Loop (Female)

Photo: Guinness World Records Limited

Kimberly Mink (USA) spun a 76 ft. 2 in. (23.21 m) loop around herself at Jerome High School in Jerome, Idaho, on January 25, 2003.

Did You Know?
Mink's entire family participates in The Rhinestone Roper Show where they perform trick roping, knife throwing, bullwhip cracking, and fancy horse tricks.

CHECK THIS OUT!

Kimberly Mink (United States) holds the world record for the Largest Trick Roping Loop by a Female. But she's not the only one in her family with an aptitude for performing. Her son, Cody Lamb (United States) was an 11-year-old cowboy from Jerome, Idaho, when he broke the world record for Youngest Person to Win the Wild West Arts' Texas Skip Race.

Texas skip racing is a type of trick roping. Trick roping has been around for a long time. It is done for fun, entertainment, and competition. To do the Texas skip, performers spin a lasso and make a wide loop. They move the loop from side to side and skip through it as they race.

Trick roping was losing popularity at the beginning of the 20th century. Now, trick roping is becoming popular again!

 **ACTIVITIES**

1. What is the relationship between Kimberly Mink and Cody Lamb?

   a. Mink is Lamb's sister.

   b. Mink is Lamb's aunt.

   c. Mink is Lamb's mother.

   d. Mink is Lamb's neighbor.

2. Read the following statements. Circle *true* or *false*.

   Mink's family has talented performers.

                           true   false

   Texas skip involves spinning a lasso.

                           true   false

   Mink has an award for trick rope jumping.

                           true   false

3. What does *aptitude* mean?

   a. dislike

   b. luck

   c. dull

   d. skill

4. Idaho borders six states. List those states here. Use a map to help you.

   1. _____   4. _____

   2. _____   5. _____

   3. _____   6. _____

5. Mink's family is a famiy of performers. Imagine that you and your family are performers. What might your family win awards for?

   _____

   _____

Fastest 100-Meter Hurdles Wearing Swim Fins (Individual, Female)

Photo: Guinness World Records Limited

In Auckland, New Zealand, on August 24, 2009, Veronica Torr (New Zealand) completed the 100-meter hurdles wearing swim fins in 19.278 seconds.

Did You Know?

Ben Franklin was an expert swimmer. At age 11, he invented swim fins shaped like lily pads to increase his speed in the water.

ACTIVITIES

1. Imagine you had to wear swim fins all day long at school. What activities would be the most fun? What would be the most challenging?

   _____

   _____

2. If you wanted to jump 12 hurdles in 45 seconds, how long would it take to complete each hurdle?

   _____

Most Consecutive Texas Style Skips

Photo: Guinness World Records Limited

On March 11, 2003, at the National Convention of the Wild West Arts Club in Las Vegas, Nevada, Andrew Rotz (USA) completed 11,123 consecutive Texas skips. The attempt took 3 hours 10 minutes to complete.

Did You Know?

Rotz practiced two hours a day for two years in order to achieve this record.

ACTIVITIES

1. Make a loop in a jump rope or a shoestring. Practice swinging the loop and using it to grab objects. Write what you were able to pick up.

_____

2. Rodeos celebrate cowboys and the Old West. Circle rodeo events you would like to try.

horse riding   **goat tail tying**

cattle roping   **barrel obstacle course**

steer wrestling   **bull riding**

Longest Time Controlling a Soccer Ball While Lying Down

Photo: Guinness World Records Limited

On November 24, 2007, Tomas Lundman (Sweden) controlled a soccer ball while lying down for 10 minutes 4 seconds at the Nordstan Shopping Mall in Gothenburg, Sweden.

Did You Know?
The elastic in Italian soccer player Giuseppe Meazza's shorts broke while he was taking a penalty shot during a semifinal match in the 1938 World Cup.

ACTIVITIES

1. How many times can you bounce a ball on your feet, hands, and body while you are lying down?

_____

2. For how many seconds did Lundman control the soccer ball?

_____

3. How many more seconds would be needed to set a record of 11 minutes?

_____

Fastest 40 Meters by a Human Wheelbarrow

Photo: Guinness World Records Limited

Adrian Rodriguez (Mexico) and Sergiy Vetrogonov (Ukraine) completed a 131.23 ft. (40 m) dash as a human wheelbarrow in 17 seconds. The record was completed in Helsinki, Finland, on November 12, 2009, in celebration of Guinness World Records Day.

Did You Know?

The Largest Human Wheelbarrow Race had 1,044 participants, or 522 pairs.

ACTIVITIES

1. Play human wheelbarrow with a friend. How many seconds does it take you to cross the room inside or cross the yard outside?

   _____

2. Which do you like better—running on your hands as the wheelbarrow or running on your feet as the operator?

   _____

3. About how far could the wheelbarrow team have traveled in one minute?

   _____

Largest Skateboard

Photo: Guinness World Records Limited

Rob Dyrdek (USA) has a skateboard that measures 36 ft. 7 in. (11.14 m) long, 8 ft. 8 in. (2.63 m) wide, and 3 ft. 7.5 in. (1.10 m) high. It was unveiled on February 25, 2009, in Los Angeles, California.

Did You Know?

This skateboard can be ridden, but four or five people have to stand together on one side to make it turn.

CHECK THIS OUT!

Most skateboards are not much longer than your arm. They are just big enough for one person. But not this skateboard! In 2009, Rob Dyrdek (United States) built a skateboard that is about as long as three cars!

Dyrdek built the board on his reality TV show. The show was called *Rob Dyrdek's Fantasy Factory*. Dyrdek's giant skateboard looks just like a regular skateboard. The difference is its size. It is big enough for many people to ride at once. It has even been ridden during parades.

Dyrdek has loved skateboards since he was a boy. He started riding when he was 12. A few years later, he turned pro. Today, Dyrdek wants to encourage young riders. That is why he has helped build skateboard parks across the country. Dyrdek makes sure that the parks are safe, legal, and, of course, fun.

ACTIVITIES

1. Dyrdek built the world's Largest Skateboard

   a. in his garage.

   b. on a playground.

   c. on his TV show.

   d. in Ohio.

2. Dyrdek began riding a skateboard when he was an adult. True or false? Circle your answer.

   true   **false**

3. In the passage on page 118, *fantasy* means "a product of the imagination." What would be an antonym of *fantasy*?

   _____

   _____

4. Skateboarding is a sport that requires riding on something. Name three other sports that require riding and tell what is being ridden.

   1. _____

   2. _____

   3. _____

5. Design your own reality TV show. Tell what the show would be about and who would star in it.

   _____

   _____

   _____

Most Double Dutch Rope Skips in One Minute

Photo: Guinness World Records Limited

On May 3, 2009, Nobuyoshi Ando (Japan) completed 202 double Dutch rope skips in one minute at the Double Dutch Harbor Festival in Tokyo, Japan.

Did You Know?

The first double Dutch tournament was held on February 14, 1974. Nearly 600 students participated from fifth, sixth, seventh, and eighth grades.

ACTIVITIES

1. Ask your mother or grandmother to teach you a jump rope rhyme from her childhood. Write the name of the rhyme.

_____

2. Write a friend's name to complete this jump rope rhyme.

   I like coffee. I like tea.

   I like _____ to jump in with me!

3. How many times can you jump rope in one minute?

_____

Fastest Speed for a Surfboard Towed by a Car

Photo: Guinness World Records Limited

On February 2, 2007, Ben Collins towed Stephanie Rowsell (both UK) with a car while she was riding a surfboard on Pendine Beach, Carmarthenshire, United Kingdom. The surfboard reached 36 mph (57.93 km/h).

Did You Know?

The Loews Coronado Bay Resort hosts an annual Surf Dog Competition in San Diego, California, where dogs catch awesome waves!

ACTIVITIES

1. Circle your favorite ways to ride the waves at the beach.

   boogie board   **surfboard**

   paddleboard   **kayak**

   motorboat   **sailboat**

2. You may not have surfed the waves, but you have probably surfed the Internet! Write the name of your favorite Web site and explain why you like it.

_____

Most Consecutive Skateboard Frontside Ollies (Half-Pipe)

Photo: Guinness World Records Limited

On September 20, 2008, Keith Baldassare (USA) performed 348 frontside ollies (half-pipe) in a row in Merritt Island, Florida.

ACTIVITIES

1. What can you do 348 times in a row?

   _____

2. The ollie skateboard trick was named after Alan "Ollie" Gelfand. What trick should be named after you?

   _____

3. What is $\frac{1}{3}$ of 348?

   _____

Most Overall Points Waterskiing (Women)

Photo: Guinness World Records Limited

On July 17, 2009, in Santa Rosa, California, Regina Jaquess (USA) earned 2,934.36 points during a waterskiing competition.

Did You Know?

The American Water Ski Association was founded in 1939. The first national championships were held the same year.

ACTIVITIES

1. Make up a point system for playing a game with a friend. For example, if you are playing cards, each card won might be worth 10 points. Write what you played and how many points you scored during the game.

_____

_____

2. How many more points would Jaquess need to earn 3,000 points?

_____

Largest Snowboard

Photo: Guinness World Records Limited

A snowboard measuring 32 ft. 9.7 in. (10 m) long and 7 ft. (2.15 m) wide was presented on March 18, 2007, in Flumserberg, Switzerland.

Did You Know?

Snowboarding combines surfing, skateboarding, and skiing. It first appeared at the 1998 Olympic Games with the giant slalom and the half-pipe.

ACTIVITIES

1. One story of a building is about 10 feet tall. About how many stories tall is the Largest Snowboard?

   _____

2. Write *snow* to complete each compound word.

   _____man   _____suit

   _____cone   _____ball

   _____mobile   _____plow

Photo: Guinness World Records Limited

BAFFLING WONDERS

Photo: Guinness World Records Limited

Orange Nose Push (Fastest Mile)

Photo: Guinness World Records Limited

In 2007, Ashrita Furman (USA) pushed an orange with his nose for a distance of one mile in 22 minutes 41 seconds.

Did You Know?
Since 1979, Furman has set more than 60 world records.

ACTIVITIES

1. Set a timer for one minute. Using your nose, how far can you push something small and round (like a ball or an orange) in that time? Write your answer in feet.

2. Your body needs vitamin C to make proteins and to keep your bones and teeth strong. Circle your favorite sources of vitamin C.

limes	grapefruit	broccoli
strawberries	oranges	lemons
cantaloupes	tomatoes	green peppers

Fastest Half Marathon in an Animal Costume (Male)

Photo: Guinness World Records Limited

Steven Townhill (UK) ran a half marathon in 1 hour 54 minutes 20 seconds while dressed as an emu on September 20, 2009.

Did You Know?
Emus are flightless birds that live only in Australia. They are the second largest birds after ostriches.

ACTIVITIES

1. Emus can run 30 miles per hour! A half marathon is about 13 miles long. At top speed, what part of an hour would it take an emu to complete the race? Round to the nearest hundredth.

_____

2. Australia is both a country and a continent. Look at a world map. Circle the primary direction you think you would travel from your home for the shortest trip to Australia.

north   south   east   west

GUINNESS WORLD RECORDS™

Largest Pie (Pumpkin)

Photo: Guinness World Records Limited

The largest pumpkin pie weighed 2,020 lb. (916.25 kg) and was 12 ft. 1 in. (3.7 m) long. It was made in Ohio on October 8, 2005.

Did You Know?
In 1863, President Abraham Lincoln declared an official Thanksgiving holiday to be celebrated each November.

ACTIVITIES

With adult help, make a small pumpkin pie in a cup!

For the crust: Crush three graham cracker squares. Mix with two teaspoons sugar and one tablespoon soft butter. Press in the bottom of a wide cup.

For the filling: Mix one tablespoon instant vanilla pudding mix, $\frac{1}{4}$ teaspoon pumpkin pie spice, three teaspoons canned pumpkin, and $\frac{1}{3}$ cup cold milk. Pour over crust.

Refrigerate for one hour. Top with whipped cream. How did your small pie taste?

Most Dominoes Stacked on Single Piece

Photo: Guinness World Records Limited

Maximilian Poser (Germany) stacked 1,002 dominoes on a single domino in Berlin, Germany, on February 6, 2009.

Did You Know?
The pieces used to set the record were not ordinary dominoes, but special ones designed for toppling competitions.

ACTIVITIES

1. How many blocks can you stack on a single block?

_____

2. Count to 100 while a friend times you. Multiply by 10 to find out how long it would take to count to 1,000. Write the time in minutes and seconds.

_____

3. Would you rather stack dominoes or knock them down? Explain your answer.

_____

Largest Restaurant

Photo: Guinness World Records Limited

On May 15, 2008, the Bawabet Dimashq Restaurant (Damascus Gate Restaurant) was named the world's largest restaurant. The restaurant is owned by Shaker Al Samman in Damascus, Syria, and has 6,014 seats.

Did You Know?
The restaurant cost $40 million to build.

CHECK THIS OUT!

Do you like going to restaurants? Many people enjoy dining out. But you've probably never been to a restaurant as large as this one!

The Bawabet Dimashq Restaurant, also called the *Damascus Gate Restaurant*, opened in 2002. The family-owned business offers a variety of meals to choose from in six separate types of cuisine: Indian, Chinese, Gulf-Arab, Iranian, Middle Eastern, and Syrian. Everyone should be able to find something to like!

During the busy summer months, up to 1,800 people are employed at the restaurant. It has an outdoor seating area that is available throughout the year, except during November, December, and January. The restaurant also has beautiful décor with waterfalls and fountains.

ACTIVITIES

1. During which months is the outdoor seating area not available?

   a. June, July, and August

   b. October, November, and December

   c. January, February, and March

   d. November, December, and January

2. What does *cuisine* mean? What is your favorite type of cuisine?

   _____

   _____

3. Circle the types of food you have eaten.

   Indian   **Chinese**

   Gulf-Arab   **Iranian**

   Middle Eastern   **Syrian**

4. The world's Largest Restaurant has 6,014 seats. If the restaurant only has tables of four, how many tables are there? Round to the nearest whole number.

   _____

5. The restaurant has beautiful décor with waterfalls and a moat. True or false? Circle your answer.

                       true   **false**

6. Pretend you are opening a restaurant. You need to create a menu! Name five main courses and five desserts you would offer to your guests.

   Main Courses   **Desserts**

   _____   _____

   _____   _____

   _____   _____

   _____   _____

   _____   _____

Farthest Grape Spitting Distance

Photo: Guinness World Records Limited

Anders Rasmussen (Norway) spat a grape 28 ft. 7.25 in. (8.72 m) on September 4, 2004.

Did You Know?
The Mozambique spitting cobra can eject venom up to 8 ft. away.

ACTIVITIES

1. The salivary glands in your mouth secrete up to four pints of saliva each day. Eight pints equal one gallon. How many gallons of saliva do you produce each week? Use a fraction in your answer.

_____

2. A dry tongue can't taste food well. Try it! Dry your tongue with a napkin and taste some food. Next, try tasting the food with a wet tongue. Describe the difference.

_____

_____

Largest Pack of Playing Cards

Photo: Guinness World Records Limited

The largest pack of playing cards measured 3 ft. 4 in. (101.6 cm) tall and 2 ft. 5 in. (73.6 cm) wide. The cards, made by Dan Bliss (USA), were displayed in 2005.

Did You Know?
A deck of playing cards can be randomized with five good shuffles.

ACTIVITIES

1. Give the height and width of each card in inches.

   _____

2. Multiply your two answers to #1. Give the area of each card in square inches.

   _____

3. Divide your answer to #2 by 144 (or 12^2). Give the area of each card in square feet. Round to the nearest tenth.

   _____

133

Tallest Chocolate Fountain

Photo: Guinness World Records Limited

The tallest chocolate fountain is 26 ft. 3 in. (8 m) tall and circulates 4,409 lb. (2 metric tons) of chocolate at a rate of 120 quarts per minute. It is displayed in Las Vegas, Nevada.

Did You Know?
The ancient Mayans may have used chocolate as a form of currency.

ACTIVITIES

1. An average pitcher holds two quarts of liquid. How many pitchers of chocolate does the fountain circulate each minute?

   _____

2. Give the difference between your height and the height of the fountain.

   _____

3. What is your favorite chocolate treat?

   _____

Largest Bottle of Cooking Oil

Photo: Guinness World Records Limited

The largest bottle of cooking oil stands 16 ft. 8 in. (5.12 m) tall and contains 706.54 gal. (3,212 L) of camellia oil. It was displayed in Guangdong Province, China, in 2009.

Did You Know?
The weight of the empty bottle was 4,801.6 lb. (2,178 kg).

ACTIVITIES

1. Over 1.3 billion people live in China. Write zeros in the spaces below to show this number.

    1, 3 _____ _____, _____ _____ _____, _____ _____ _____

2. About $\frac{1}{7}$ of China's population uses camellia oil, or tea seed oil, for cooking. How many people is this? (Hint: Use your answer to #1 and a calculator to find this very large number. Round to the nearest whole number.)

    _____

3. What kind of cooking oil is used in your home?

    _____

Largest Ice Cream Cone

Photo: Guinness World Records Limited

The largest ice cream cone measured 9 ft. 2.63 in. (2.81 m) in height and was achieved by Mirco Della Vecchia and Andrea Andrighetti (both Italy) during an event in Rimini, Italy, on January 22, 2011.

Did You Know?

Making gelato is essentially the same thing as making homemade ice cream.

CHECK THIS OUT!

Mirco Della Vecchia (Italy), the man in charge of creating the world's Largest Ice Cream Cone, is no stranger to Guinness World Records. In 2009, he set a record for the Largest Chocolate Sculpture, which he then broke again in April 2010 with a chocolate sculpture weighing 10,736 pounds!

For this attempt, Vecchia led a team of seven people in making the gelato. *Gelato* is an Italian word for "ice cream." It was made with fresh milk, sugar, cream, mascarpone, and aromatic cake paste. The preparation of the gelato took the team about 30 hours of work.

The ice cream cone was decorated with 2,000 round wafer biscuits. Gelato scoops were frozen for 24 hours and then placed in the cone and decorated with black cherries and chocolate.

ACTIVITIES

1. Complete the crossword puzzle with words you read on page 136.

Across

2. The gelato took this many hours to prepare.

4. Month in which Vecchia set the record for the world's Largest Ice Cream Cone.

5. The man in charge of creating the world's Largest Ice Cream Cone.

7. The Largest Ice Cream Cone was decorated with chocolate and _____ .

8. The Italian word for ice cream.

9. The cone was decorated with 2,000 of these.

Down

1. The scoops of gelato were _____ for 24 hours.

3. The gelato was made with fresh milk, mascarpone, cream, aromatic cake paste, and this.

6. Vecchia's first world record was for the Largest _____ Sculpture.

2. An average car weighs 4,000 pounds. Does the world's Largest Ice Cream Cone weigh more or less than three cars? Circle your answer.

more than three cars   **less than three cars**

3. If you could create your own brand new flavor of ice cream, what would it be?

_____

In 2010, the smallest commercially available jigsaw puzzle measured 11.65 in. (29.6 cm) wide and 8.27 in. (21 cm) tall. It was made by a Chinese company.

Photo: Guinness World Records Limited

Did You Know?

The puzzle, which has 500 pieces, shows a picture of Machu Picchu in Peru.

ACTIVITIES

1. Circle your answer. The puzzle is about the same size as:

   a bed pillow   **a cell phone**   **a sheet of printer paper**

2. Cut a picture from a magazine or print one from your computer. Write a message on the back. Then, cut up the picture to make a jigsaw puzzle. Put the pieces in an envelope and give the puzzle to a friend. Write what you did.

_____

_____

Longest Leather Belt

Photo: Guinness World Records Limited

The Almpani Brothers factory in Thessaloniki, Greece, made a leather belt 206 ft. 36 in. (62 m 91 cm) long in 2008.

Did You Know?
An average pair of jeans has seven belt loops.

ACTIVITIES

1. Would you rather hold up your pants with a belt or with suspenders? Explain your answer.

   _____

2. Batman often wears a utility belt that contains crime-fighting tools such as a camera, radio, phone, and lasso. List what you would wear on your belt if you were a superhero.

   _____   _____

   _____   _____

Largest Sandwich

Photo: Guinness World Records Limited

Wild Woody's Chill and Grill in Roseville, Michigan, made a sandwich that weighed 5,440 lb. (2,467.5 kg) in 2005.

Did You Know?
The sandwich contained bread, corned beef, lettuce, cheese, and mustard.

ACTIVITIES

1. The bread weighed 3,568 pounds. The mustard weighed 150 pounds. How much did the other ingredients weigh?

   _____

2. If the sandwich were cut into $\frac{1}{2}$-pound servings, how many people could be fed?

   _____

3. What are your favorite sandwich ingredients?

   _____

Longest Tail on a Dog

Photo: Guinness World Records Limited

The longest dog tail measured 24 in. (61 cm) long on March 30, 2011. The tail belongs to Allie, a Great Dane who lives in Indiana.

Did You Know?
Pictures of dogs resembling Great Danes can be found on ancient Egyptian monuments.

ACTIVITIES

1. Great Danes can grow to be 40 inches tall. What's the difference between your height and a Great Dane's height?

   _____

2. Each day, Great Danes require food and water, a long walk for exercise, and human companionship. How would you help care for a Great Dane?

   _____

3. What type of dog would you like to own someday?

   _____

Largest Bottle of Liquid Soap

Photo: Guinness World Records Limited

The largest bottle of liquid soap measured 15 ft. 5 in. (4.70 m) tall by 5 ft. 0.6 in. (1.54 m) wide and weighed 2,303 lb. 13 oz. (1,045 kg). The bottle, which was filled with shampoo, was produced in Jeddah, Saudi Arabia, on March 19, 2009.

Did You Know?

On average, people take 10.4-minute showers.

CHECK IT OUT!

Scrub a dub dub! It's time to get in the tub. Taking a shower or bath every day is the best way to get clean and stay clean.

When do you usually take your baths? Some people take baths in the evening, and some take them in the morning. A bath in the evening removes all the dust, grime, and sweat that you have gathered throughout the day. A bath in the morning refreshes you and makes you ready for the day ahead.

When you wash your hair, how big is your shampoo bottle? There's no way it could be as big as this one! A company in Saudi Arabia is in the record books for producing the world's Largest Bottle of Liquid Soap. It is about as tall as three people standing on each other's shoulders! Filling a bottle this size with shampoo takes an hour and a half!

ACTIVITIES

1. Filling the Largest Bottle of Liquid Soap takes

   a. 90 minutes.

   b. 60 minutes.

   c. 45 minutes.

   d. 120 minutes.

2. Ask three friends or family members how tall they are. Then, add their heights together. Would they be shorter or taller than the Largest Bottle of Liquid Soap? Circle your answer.

   shorter   **taller**

3. Unscramble words you read on page 142.

   mrige   _____

   tuds   _____

   aewts   _____

   thba   _____

   mpohsao   _____

   ohsrew   _____

   eclna   _____

4. Do you prefer taking baths or showers? Explain your answer.

   _____

   _____

5. The average person uses 12.4 gallons of water to take a shower. Name a way you could use less water when taking a shower.

   _____

6. Find Saudi Arabia on a map. Name two countries that border Saudi Arabia.

   1. _____   2. _____

Largest Disco Ball

Photo: Guinness World Records Limited

The largest mirrored disco ball measured 24 ft. 1.3 in. (7.35 m) in diameter. It was made by Raf Frateur and was displayed at a party in Antwerp, Belgium, on July 20, 2007.

Did You Know?
The ball was made from approximately 80,000 small mirrors.

ACTIVITIES

1. The diameter of the disco ball was about 24 feet. If you know the diameter of a circle (d), you can calculate its circumference (C), or distance around the outside. Pi (π) has a value of 3.14. Use this equation to find the circumference of the Largest Disco Ball in feet: $\pi \times d = C$.

2. The number π goes on forever. Computers have calculated it to one trillion digits past the decimal point. Research and write the first 10 digits of π.

Longest Chain of Neckties (Team)

Photo: Guinness World Records Limited

A chain of 8,695 neckties was created by the Get Knotted Tie Challenge in Bathurst, NSW, Australia, on February 11, 2010.

Did You Know?
The chain of ties had a length of 7.71 mi. (12.406 km).

ACTIVITIES

1. If $\frac{1}{5}$ of the ties had polka dots, how many ties had some other pattern?

_____

2. Decorate the bow tie with colors and designs.

Largest Cardboard Box

Photo: Guinness World Records Limited

The largest cardboard box measured 20 ft. 1.2 in. (6.12 m) wide, 46 ft. 1.2 in. (14.05 m) long, and 9 ft. 0.3 in. (2.75 m) high. It was presented at the Rose Bowl in Pasadena, California, in 2009.

Did You Know?
Corrugated cardboard boxes are used to ship nearly 90% of all products in the United States.

ACTIVITIES

Forts can include doors, windows, tunnels, secret rooms, lookout posts, and escape hatches. Describe the fort you and your friends would make from the world's Largest Cardboard Box. Write how you would use the fort after it is built.

_____

_____

_____

_____

Fastest Half Marathon Dressed as a Vegetable

Photo: Guinness World Records Limited

Nick Lodge (UK) ran a half marathon while dressed as a carrot in 1 hour 37 minutes 21 seconds. He ran in London, United Kingdom, to raise money for a children's charity.

Did You Know?
Eating too many carrots can cause your skin to turn yellowish-orange.

ACTIVITIES

1. Circle your favorite way to eat carrots.

in chicken soup   **carrot juice**

in a fresh salad   **carrot sticks with dip**

in a stir-fry   **carrot cake**

2. Carrots are orange because they contain beta carotene. List four more things in nature that are orange.

_____ _____

_____ _____

Largest Chocolate Bar

Photo: Guinness World Records Limited

The largest chocolate bar weighed 9,722.39 lb. (4,410 kg) and was made by Armenian-Canadian JV "Grand Candy" Co. Ltd., in Yerevan, Armenia, on September 10, 2010.

Did You Know?

The word *chocolate* comes from the Aztec word *cacahuatl* or *xocolatl*, which means "bitter water."

CHECK THIS OUT!

Chocolate can come in many different varieties, such as dark chocolate, milk chocolate, or white chocolate. You can eat chocolate in cookies, cakes, muffins, or brownies. Some people even put chocolate in chili!

In 2010, a candy company wanted to use chocolate as a way to celebrate its 10th anniversary. What better way to do that than by creating the world's Largest Chocolate Bar? The bar was 18.37 feet long, 9.02 feet wide, and 9.84 inches tall.

Making this chocolate bar was no small feat. It took 3,029 pounds of sugar, as well as cocoa liquor, cocoa powder, cocoa butter, and vanilla. It took 48 hours to mix the chocolate glaze, including five hours to roast and grind the cocoa beans.

ACTIVITIES

1. What is your favorite way to eat chocolate?

_____

2. The bar was 18.37 feet long, 9.02 feet wide, and 9.84 feet tall. True or false? Circle your answer.

     true   **false**

3. How long did it take to mix the chocolate glaze?

   a. 48 hours

   b. 43 hours

   c. 5 hours

   d. 53 hours

4. A candy company celebrates its 10th anniversary in 2010. In what year did the company start?

_____

5. Circle five words you read on page 148 to complete the word search. Use the word bank to help you.

> **chocolate   cookies   muffins   brownies   cakes**

```
F   Z   P   M   D   I   X   Q   O
L   C   B   T   C   X   Q   H   G
Z   A   R   M   W   K   D   J   V
K   X   O   C   C   W   C   B   E
R   H   W   H   O   E   A   G   M
T   H   N   O   O   O   K   R   U
X   D   I   C   K   C   E   A   F
X   F   E   O   I   Y   S   N   F
M   E   S   L   E   N   N   Q   I
J   Y   U   A   S   S   T   E   N
P   P   F   T   U   G   N   Y   S
N   G   F   E   C   X   D   F   A
```

Heaviest Shoes Walked In

Photo: Guinness World Records Limited

On November 18, 2010, Ashrita Furman (USA) walked in shoes that weighed 323 lb. (146.5 kg) at Potters Fields Park in London, United Kingdom.

Did You Know?
Many runners prefer super lightweight shoes (less than 1 lb. per pair).

ACTIVITIES

1. The pair of shoes Furman wore weighed 323 pounds. How much did each shoe weigh?

   _____

2. How heavy are the shoes you usually wear? Use a bathroom scale to find out.

   _____

3. About how many pairs of your shoes would equal 323 pounds?

   _____

Largest Gingerbread Man

Photo: Guinness World Records Limited

The largest gingerbread man weighed 1,435 lb. 3 oz. (651 kg) and was made in Oslo, Norway, on November 9, 2009.

Did You Know?

The giant gingerbread man was baked in one piece. His ingredients included flour, sugar, cinnamon, ginger, and salt.

ACTIVITIES

1. What would you use to decorate the giant gingerbread man?

_____

2. In the story "The Gingerbread Man," a freshly baked gingerbread man escapes and runs away so no one can eat him. Where would a gingerbread man hide in your house or neighborhood?

_____

3. What special treat does your family make for a holiday?

_____

Largest Admission Ticket

Photo: Guinness World Records Limited

The largest admission ticket was 56.25 in. (142 cm) wide and 19.69 in. (50 cm) tall. It was created by Canada's National Arts Centre in 2007.

Did You Know?
A few people have paid the Russian space agency up to $50 million for a ticket to visit the International Space Station.

ACTIVITIES

1. What is the area of the world's Largest Admission Ticket in square inches? Round to the nearest hundredth.

   _____

2. Put on a play or performance for friends and family. Use large paper to make giant tickets for your show. Write what you did.

   _____

   _____

Longest Ice Cream Dessert

Photo: Guinness World Records Limited

The Kids Club (USA) in Brunswick, Georgia, prepared an ice cream sundae 130 ft. 6 in. (39.77 m) long on November 12, 2009.

Did You Know?

The sundae was made from vanilla ice cream, chocolate sauce, and peanuts. It weighed 169 lb. (76.7 kg).

ACTIVITIES

1. If the sundae were divided into six-inch servings, how many people could have some?

   _____

2. The words *desert* ("a dry place") and *dessert* ("a sweet treat") are frequently confused. So are *sundae* ("ice cream with toppings") and *Sunday* ("the first day of the week"). Write definitions for these frequently confused words.

   piece: _____

   peace: _____

Largest Salad

Photo: Guinness World Records Limited

The largest salad weighed 29,579 lb. (13,417 kg), measured 82 ft. (25 m) in length, 11 ft. 2 in. (3 m 40 cm) in width, and 10.2 in. (26 cm) in depth. It was measured in Crete, Greece, on June 19, 2010.

Did You Know?
Darker green lettuce leaves are more nutritious than lighter green leaves.

CHECK THIS OUT!

Salads can be very healthy meals. They are a great way to eat lots of vegetables to give you lots of energy. Just don't go overboard on the dressing!

You could say that the world's Largest Salad went overboard. It weighed over 29,000 pounds! The salad consisted of tomatoes, cucumbers, onions, green peppers, and feta cheese. It was marinated in olive oil, oregano, and salt. The salad was made by 600–700 volunteers who had all been trained in cutting vegetables and handling food.

After the record attempt, the salad was given to locals and tourists. A large amount was also donated to many shelters across Crete.

1. Circle the toppings you would put on your perfect salad.

        tomatoes   **croutons**

        cucumbers   **broccoli**

        carrots   **onions**

        green pepper   **shredded cheese**

        bacon bits   **peas**

2. There are many types of salads, such as macaroni salad and Caesar salad. How many more types of salads can you name?

_____   _____   _____

_____   _____   _____

3. What was not done with the salad after the record attempt?

a. It was given to locals.

b. It was given to tourists.

c. It was sold at markets.

d. It was donated to shelters.

4. It took 700–800 volunteers to make the world's Largest Salad. True or false? Circle your answer.

                    true   **false**

5. The world's Largest Pancake weighed 6,614 pounds when it was made in 1994. Which weighed more? Circle your answer.

        Largest Pancake   **Largest Salad**

6. Why do you think the salad was donated to shelters across Crete?

_____

_____

_____

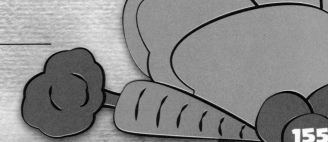

Largest Wave Pool

The largest wave pool covers 146,388.6 sq. ft. or 3.36 acres (13,600 m²). It can be found at Siam Park in Bangkok, Thailand.

Photo: Guinness World Records Limited

Did You Know?

According to the World Waterpark Association, the wave pool holds 2,199,691.52 gal. (8,326,738.2 L) of water.

ACTIVITIES

1. Wave pools have been called *artificial seas*. Write two ways wave pools are like oceans.

_____   _____

2. Write two ways oceans are different from wave pools.

_____   _____

3. What do you like to do best at a waterpark?

_____

_____

Largest Box of Chocolates

Photo: Guinness World Records Limited

A Thorntons Moments box of chocolates weighed 3,725 lb. (1,690 kg) in London, United Kingdom, on April 2, 2008.

Did You Know?

Chocolate contains a chemical, theobromine, which can be poisonous to dogs and other animals.

ACTIVITIES

Chocolate is made from cacao beans that grow on tropical trees near Earth's equator. Number these steps from 1–5 to show the correct order for making chocolate.

_____ Paste is mixed with sugar.

_____ Cacao beans are harvested from tropical trees.

_____ Cacao beans are ground into paste.

_____ Cacao beans are roasted and shelled.

_____ Sweetened paste is shaped into candies.

Largest Horseshoe

Photo: Guinness World Records Limited

The largest hand-forged horseshoe measured 1 ft. 10 in. (56 cm) tall and 2 ft. (61.5 cm) wide. It was created at the international blacksmith festival Ferraculum in Ybbsitz, Austria, in 2008.

Did You Know?

A blacksmith creates objects by forging (using tools to hammer, bend, and cut) metal.

ACTIVITIES

1. Horseshoes is the game of throwing U-shaped pieces toward a stake. What is your favorite game to play in the yard?

   _____

2. Horseshoes—along with ladybugs, pennies, elephants, rainbows, crickets, wishing wells, and four-leaf clovers—are thought to bring good luck. Draw your favorite good luck symbol.

Largest Muffin

Photo: Guinness World Records Limited

The largest muffin weighed 195.55 lb. (88.7 kg) and measured 2 ft. 7 in. (79 cm) in diameter and 1 ft. 6 in. (45.5 cm) in height. It was made by master baker Gerhard Hinz (Germany) in 2010.

Did You Know?

The muffin contained wheat flour, butter, and lots of marshmallows.

ACTIVITIES

1. Circle your favorite muffin flavor.

   chocolate chip   **banana nut**   **apple cinnamon**

   carrot cake   **blueberry**   **lemon poppy seed**

2. Give the height of the Largest Muffin in inches.

   _____

3. The muffin used about 42 pounds of butter. How many $\frac{1}{4}$-pound sticks of butter were needed for the recipe?

   _____

Longest Line of Pies

The longest line of pies measured 530 ft. 8 in. (161.75 m) long and was achieved by Randall D. Fox (USA) as part of the Chastain Park Arts Festival, in Atlanta, Georgia, on October 18, 2009.

Photo: Guinness World Records Limited

Did You Know?
The average American eats six slices of pie per year.

CHECK THIS OUT!

Pumpkin pies are a popular dessert for the fall and wintertime. You can often find people eating pumpkin pies on Thanksgiving Day, after a filling meal of turkey, mashed potatoes, stuffing, and corn.

If you were in Atlanta, Georgia, in October 2009, you might have also found pumpkin pies lined up for over 530 feet! The organizers of the Chastain Park Arts Festival decided to attempt a world record. They created a line of 800 eight-inch pies that made it into the record books!

But those aren't the only pumpkin pies to set a world record. The world's Largest Pumpkin Pie consisted of 1,212 pounds of canned pumpkin, 109 gallons of evaporated milk, 2,796 eggs, 7 pounds of salt, 14.5 pounds of cinnamon, and 525 pounds of sugar. It weighed 3,699 pounds!

1. The record for the Longest Line of Pies was set in Ohio. True or false? Circle your answer.

   true   **false**

2. Is 530 feet of pies more or less than a mile? Circle your answer.

   more than a mile   **less than a mile**

3. If the average American eats six slices of pie per year, how many slices does the average American eat each month?

   a. one slice

   b. two slices

   c. 12 slices

   d. half a slice

4. The Longest Line of Pies consisted of 800 eight-inch pies. What is 800 multiplied by 8?

   _____

5. Unscramble words you read on page 160.

   mpiunpk   _____

   redests   _____

   khnavniggTsi   _____

   rtkeuy   _____

6. Describe your favorite Thanksgiving meal. What are your favorite things to eat on the holiday? Do you typically eat a slice of pumpkin pie?

   _____

   _____

   _____

   _____

Largest Human Awareness Ribbon

© RANIA A. RAZEK

Photo: Guinness World Records Limited

As part of Breast Cancer Awareness Month in October 2010, 3,952 women formed a human awareness ribbon in Jeddah, Saudi Arabia.

Did You Know?

The event was organized by Her Royal Highness Princess Reema bint Bandar bin Sultan Al-Saud.

ACTIVITIES

1. How many more people would need to participate to bring the record to 5,000 people?

_____

2. What event in your community has helped to raise awareness about an important issue?

_____

3. Look at a world map to find Saudi Arabia in the Middle East. What two bodies of water border this large country?

Longest Line of Sandwiches

Photo: Guinness World Records Limited

The longest line of sandwiches measured 8,750 ft. 4.91 in. (2,667.13 m) long. It was presented at the Dubai Outlet Mall in Dubai, United Arab Emirates, on September 7, 2010.

Did You Know?

The line was formed from 11,000 individual sandwiches made with cream cheese, cucumbers, tomatoes, and olives.

ACTIVITIES

1. There are 5,280 feet in one mile. Was the Longest Line of Sandwiches shorter or longer than one mile? Circle your answer.

   shorter   **longer**

2. Imagine you shared a three foot-long sub sandwich with your family. Each person's portion would be how many inches long?

   _____

3. What is your favorite vegetable to put on a sandwich?

   _____

Largest Hula-Hoop Spun

Photo: Guinness World Records Limited

On September 9, 2010, at Hillcrest High School in New York City, Ashrita Furman (USA) spun a Hula-Hoop with a diameter of 16 ft. 6.7 in. (5.04 m). He spun it $3\frac{3}{4}$ times in a row.

Did You Know?
The Hula-Hoop was made of carbon fiber.

ACTIVITIES

1. The Hula-Hoop had a diameter of over 16 feet. That length is about how many times your height?

_____

2. Classic toys are simple, low-tech toys that children have played with for generations. Read the list of toys and the approximate years they were invented. Circle your favorites.

yo-yo (1929)	**Frisbee**® (1957)	**Hula-Hoop**® (1958)
pogo stick (1919)	**Slinky**® (1945)	**Lincoln Logs**® (1916)
Twister® (1966)	**Play-Doh**® (1955)	**Rollerblades**® (1990)

Longest Skewer of Kebab Meat

Photo: Guinness World Records Limited

The largest skewer of kebab meat weighed 8,866 lb. 15 oz. (4,022 kg). The record was set by Zith Catering Equipment Ltd. and the municipality of Pafos, Cyprus, in 2008.

Did You Know?

Cyprus is an island nation in the Mediterranean Sea.

ACTIVITIES

1. Write the name of a Middle Eastern country.

_____

2. In the Middle East, gyros are a popular fast food. Kebab meat is slowly roasted on a spit, then sliced and stuffed into pita bread along with tasty toppings. Circle gyro ingredients you would like to eat.

lamb kebab	lettuce	onion
beef kebab	pita bread	tomato
pork kebab	cold tzatziki yogurt sauce	

Largest Playing Card Structure

Photo: Guinness World Records Limited

The largest playing card structure was a replica of The Venetian® Macao, The Plaza™ Macao, and Sands Macao. It measured 34 ft. 1.05 in. (10.39 m) long, 9 ft. 5.39 in. (2.88 m) tall, and 11 ft. 7.37 in. (3.54 m) wide. It was created by Bryan Berg (USA) in Macau, China, on March 10, 2010.

Did You Know?
Red is considered a lucky color in China. Perhaps that is why the Chinese flag is predominantly red!

CHECK THIS OUT!

What kinds of games do you like to play with playing cards? The possibilities are almost endless. There are dozens of games for all different ages. Some games allow you to play with a large group of people, while other games you can play all by yourself.

Bryan Berg (United States) used playing cards for something besides games. He used them to build the Largest Playing Card Structure! This structure was a replica of three resort hotels in China, and stretched over 34 feet long. It took Berg 44 days to complete the entire thing!

A standard deck of playing cards has 52 cards. In order to create this large structure, Berg used 218,792 cards! That's about 4,208 decks of cards!

1. If each deck of cards cost $1.99, about how much money would Berg need to buy the cards for the Largest Playing Card Structure?

   a. $8,358

   b. $43,525.28

   c. $43,525

   d. $8,373.92

2. If Berg completed the structure on March 10, during which month did he begin building it? Circle your answer.

   January   **February**

3. What does *replica* mean?

   a. copy

   b. mistake

   c. original

   d. picture

4. Card games are fun. Do you agree or disagree with this statement? Explain your answer.

   _____

   _____

5. Finish the sentence.

   China is on the continent of _____.

6. China has people speaking almost 300 different languages. Do you know any words in another language? List as many as you can.

   _____   _____   _____

   _____   _____   _____

   _____   _____   _____

Largest Slab of Fudge

Photo: Guinness World Records Limited

The Northwest Fudge Factory made a slab of fudge weighing 5,760 lb. (2.61 metric tons) in Levack, Ontario, Canada, on October 23, 2010.

Did You Know?

The fudge took one week to make, and contained portions of vanilla, chocolate, and maple flavors.

ACTIVITIES

Candy makers cook mixtures at high temperatures, allowing more sugar to dissolve into the candy. Fudge is heated to about 240°F. Try this experiment to see how sugar dissolves.

With adult help, put cold water in one clear glass and hot tap water in another clear glass. Stir sugar into each glass, $\frac{1}{2}$ teaspoon at a time. Count how many spoonfuls dissolve in each glass before the water is saturated, and sugar begins to collect on the bottom. Which glass of water was able to dissolve the most sugar?

Largest Beach Towel

Photo: Guinness World Records Limited

The largest beach towel measured 285 ft. 10 in. (87.14 m) long and 82 ft. 8 in. (25.20 m) wide. It was displayed at Playa de las Canteras in Las Palmas, Gran Canaria, Spain, on June 5, 2010.

Did You Know?
It took eight days to make the towel.

ACTIVITIES

1. The Largest Beach Towel was about 286 feet long and 83 feet wide. Give its area in square feet.

   _____

2. If each person were given four square feet of the towel to sit on, how many people would fit on the towel? Round to the nearest whole number.

   _____

3. What do you take with you when you go to the beach or the pool?

   _____

Longest Chain of Shoes

Photo: Guinness World Records Limited

A chain of 20,110 shoes was created by the South Main Baptist Church in Houston, Texas, on August 21, 2010.

Did You Know?

Four thousand years ago, the first shoe may have been made from a single piece of rawhide that surrounded the foot for warmth and protection.

ACTIVITIES

1. How many pairs of shoes were in the chain?

_____

2. If $\frac{1}{5}$ of the shoe pairs were children's sizes, how many pairs were adult sizes?

_____

3. Write what this old saying means to you: "Never judge people until you have walked a mile in their shoes."

_____

_____

Largest Collection of Rubber Ducks

Photo: Guinness World Records Limited

Charlotte Lee (USA) has 5,631 different rubber ducks in her collection, which she began in 1996.

Did You Know?
Lee displays her collection on glass shelves in a "duck room" at her house.

ACTIVITIES

1. What do you like to collect?

_____

2. Decorate these ducks with different colors and designs.

Largest Ant Farm

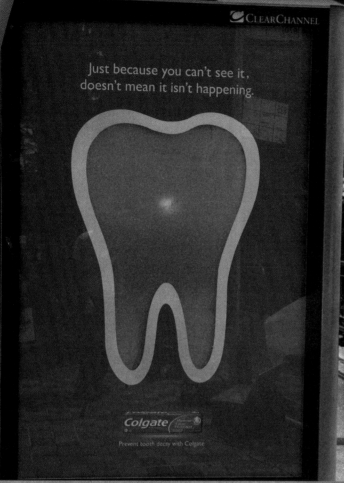

Photo: Guinness World Records Limited

The largest ant farm habitat is 3 ft. 11 in. (1.2 m) tall, 2 ft. 11 in. (0.9 m) wide, and 3 in. (0.08 m) deep. The habitat was created by Colgate Palmolive Ltd. in Singapore, Singapore, on December 28, 2008.

Did You Know?
Dentists recommend that the only safe drinks between meals are water and milk. Water and milk are less acidic and less sugary than other drinks, which means less erosion and less decay.

CHECK THIS OUT!

Taking care of your teeth is very important. You need your teeth for chewing, biting, and even talking. Once you lose your baby teeth, your adult teeth should be with you for the rest of your life, so it's important to keep them strong and healthy.

A toothpaste company in Singapore wanted to create a display to show the importance of taking care of your teeth. They decided to create an ant farm in the shape of a tooth. It was filled with toothpaste gel. About 200–300 ants were released into the habitat, and within a day, the ants had begun digging. They created mini tunnels within the gel, giving the impression that the "tooth" had cavities. The slogan on the display read, "Just because you can't see it, doesn't mean it isn't happening."

ACTIVITIES

1. Do you think the Largest Ant Farm habitat was effective in showing the importance of taking care of your teeth? Explain why or why not.

_____

_____

2. Circle ways to take care of your teeth.

eating healthy foods   **eating sugary foods**

brushing your teeth twice a day   **visiting the dentist regularly**

3. Snacks that are low in sugar are the best options for keeping your teeth strong. What are three healthy snacks?

   a. apples, cake, and candy

   b. carrots, apples, and milk

   c. apples, carrots, and cake

   d. brownies, carrots, and milk

4. Explain the slogan "Just because you can't see it, doesn't mean it isn't happening."

_____

_____

5. Do some research on Singapore and finish the sentence.

   Singapore is made up of _____ **islands.**

6. Create your own display that shows the importance of taking care of your teeth. Draw it here.

Largest Arcade Machine

Photo: Guinness World Records Limited

The largest arcade machine measured 13 ft. 6 in. (4.14 m) tall, 9 ft. 4 in. (2.84 m) deep, and 5 ft. 8 in. (1.72 m) wide. It was unveiled in Los Angeles, California, on November 9, 2007.

Did You Know?

The arcade machine weighs 1,500 lb. (680.9 kg). It can play 150 different games.

ACTIVITIES

1. Estimate how many different arcade games or video games you have played in your lifetime.

   _____

2. Write the names of your four favorite video games.

   _____   _____

   _____   _____

3. If each game costs $0.50, how much would it cost to play all 150 games?

   _____

Largest Piñata

Photo: Guinness World Records Limited

The largest piñata measured 47 ft. (14.32 m) tall, 68 ft. 7 in. (20.9 m) long, and 37 ft. 9 in. (11.5 m) wide. It was created by M&M'S® and displayed in New York City on August 4, 2011.

Did You Know?

The piñata was in the shape of an orange pretzel M&M standing on a birthday cake.

ACTIVITIES

With adult help, make a papier-mâché piñata. Blow up a balloon. Tear strips of newspaper, paper towel, or printer paper. In a disposable container, mix $\frac{1}{2}$ glue and $\frac{1}{2}$ water. Dip strips into the mixture and smooth them in 2-3 overlapping layers to cover the balloon. Remember to leave a hole at the bottom! Allow to dry for 1-2 days, pop the balloon, and then fill with candy. Tape paper over the hole, then paint or decorate. Draw a picture of your piñata.

Largest Yo-Yo

Photo: Guinness World Records Limited

The largest yo-yo was devised as part of a team problem-solving class at Bay de Noc Community College in Escanaba, Michigan, in 2010. The yo-yo weighed 1,625 lb. (738.64 kg).

Did You Know?

The yo-yo was launched by crane from a height of 100 ft. (30.48 m) and yo-yoed 38 times.

ACTIVITIES

1. The Largest Yo-Yo had a diameter (d) of 11 feet, 6 inches. Give the diameter in inches.

   _____

2. Find the distance around the yo-yo, or the circumference (C) in inches, using this equation: $3.14\ (\pi) \times d = C$.

   _____

3. Write about something you made with a group of friends.

   _____

Largest Bandage

Photo: Guinness World Records Limited

The world's largest bandage measured 141 in. (360 cm) long and 37 in. (95 cm) wide. It was created by David Martínez Fernández, Juan Luceño Montero, and Eduardo Torello Rivera (all Spain) in 2004.

Did You Know?
A first-aid kit should include bandages, antibiotic ointment, a thermometer, and a first-aid manual.

ACTIVITIES

1. If you used 15 bandages during each summer you have been alive, how many would you have used in all?

   _____

2. A minor cut or scrape heals in about 10 days. If you used a new bandage every other day, how many bandages would you use in the time it takes your cut to heal?

   _____

Longest Sandwich

Photo: Guinness World Records Limited

The longest sandwich measured 2,081 ft. (634.50 m) long and was created by Pietro Catucci and Antonio Latte (both Italy) in Taranto, Italy, on August 7, 2004.

Did You Know?

The ham sandwich is the most popular sandwich in the United States. The BLT is the second most popular.

CHECK THIS OUT!

Do you think setting a Guinness World Record would be an easy thing to do? If so, keep reading, and maybe you'll change your mind!

In 2004, Pietro Catucci and Antonio Latte (both Italy) set the record for the world's Longest Sandwich. The ingredients for the bread included 2,028.25 pounds of flour, 112.6 gallons of water, and 55.11 pounds of salt. The bread was left to rise for over 24 hours, and was then transported, half-cooked, from the oven onto tables using two cranes!

On the tables, it continued baking by using a specially created movable oven. Once cooled, it was filled with salami and mortadella and topped with mayonnaise and tuna. The sandwich weighed 34,275.22 pounds and was eaten by 19,000 people! Now, do you think it sounds easy?

ACTIVITIES

1. Build your own sandwich! Circle the items you would put on your perfect sandwich.

turkey	**cheese**	**mayonnaise**
relish	**lettuce**	**ham**
tomato	**onion**	**salami**
mustard	**pickles**	**tuna**

2. Using context clues, define *mortadella*.

   a. a type of bread

   b. another name for salami

   c. an Italian cold cut

   d. small sandwiches

3. Do you think setting a Guinness World Record would be easy to do? Explain why or why not.

   _____

   _____

4. Circle five words you read on page 178 to complete the word search. Use the word bank to help you.

bread   sandwich   salami   mortadella   tuna

```
B  S  A  N  D  W  I  C  H  F  V  T
O  A  X  A  D  N  K  H  R  G  I  U
N  L  Y  P  D  P  A  S  T  V  K  N
X  A  M  O  R  T  A  D  E  L  L  A
Q  M  O  F  I  M  K  M  X  H  G  V
W  I  Y  F  F  T  N  B  R  E  A  D
```

Longest Necktie

Photo: Guinness World Records Limited

Members of the Academia Cravatica organization made a necktie measuring 2,650 ft. (808 m) long. It was tied around the arena in Pula, Croatia, on October 18, 2003.

Did You Know?
Christo and Jeanne-Claude are known for their giant works of art. In 1983, they surrounded 11 islands near Miami, Florida, with floating fabric.

ACTIVITIES

1. There are 5,280 feet in a mile. Was the Longest Necktie longer or shorter than $\frac{1}{2}$ mile? Circle your answer.

   shorter than $\frac{1}{2}$ mile   **longer than $\frac{1}{2}$ mile**

2. There are three feet in a yard. How many yards of fabric would it take to make the Longest Necktie? Round to the nearest hundredth.

   _____

3. What giant item would you tie around a stadium?

   _____

Heaviest Dog Breed

Photo: Guinness World Records Limited

The heaviest breeds of domestic dogs are the Old English mastiff (pictured) and the Saint Bernard. The males of both species regularly weigh 170–200 lb. (77–91 kg), the weight of an average adult man.

Did You Know?

If babies grew as fast as most mastiffs do, they could weigh as much as 700 lb. (317.5 kg) by age two.

ACTIVITIES

1. Find the average weight of these dogs: an Old English mastiff (185 pounds), a Chihuahua (7 pounds), a Saint Bernard (198 pounds), and a cocker spaniel (26 pounds).

2. Would you rather own a small dog or a large dog? Explain your answer.

Tallest Costume
Worn Running in a Marathon

In 2010, Jean Paul Delacy (UK) completed a marathon in London, United Kingdom, while wearing a giraffe costume measuring 23 ft. 1 in. (7.04 m) tall.

Photo: Guinness World Records Limited

Did You Know?
Delacy finished the race ahead of a contestant carrying a giant mobile phone.

ACTIVITIES

1. Real giraffes stand up to 19 feet tall. How many inches taller was Delacy's costume?

_____

2. What type of costume might help you run faster during a race?

_____

3. What type of costume might slow you down during a race?

_____

Largest Broom (Continental)

Photo: Guinness World Records Limited

The largest broom measured 107 ft. 1 in. (32.65 m) in length. It was presented in Sint-Annaland, Netherlands, in 2006.

Did You Know?
Early brooms were made by tying straw, twigs, or cornhusks to a handle.

ACTIVITIES

1. The broom handle measured 68 feet, 5 inches. How long was the rest of the broom? Give your answer in inches.

   _____

2. Sweeping the floor, porch, or walkway is a good way to help out around the house. What chores do you do at home to help your family?

   _____

   _____

Largest Dental Caps

Photo: Guinness World Records Limited

Spike, a resident Asian elephant at the Calgary Zoo, Alberta, Canada, has dental caps that measure approximately 20 in. (50 cm) long, 5 in. (13 cm) in diameter, and weigh 29 lb. (13 kg) each.

Did You Know?
Some of the first toothbrushes were made with hair bristles from a pig's neck.

ACTIVITIES

1. What is the combined length of Spike's two dental caps? Give your answer in feet and inches.

   _____

2. Many wild elephants live south of the Sahara Desert. Look at a map. On what continent is the Sahara Desert?

   _____

3. Do you know the answer to this elephant joke: What weighs 10,000 pounds and has glass slippers?

Fastest Skateboard Speed (Standing)

The fastest skateboard speed from a standing position was 70.21 mph (113 km/h). The record was set by Douglas da Silva (Brazil) on October 20, 2007.

Did You Know?
The first outdoor skate park was constructed for skateboarders in Florida in 1976.

ACTIVITIES

1. Find out the speed limit on a highway near your home. How many miles per hour over that limit was da Silva traveling?
   Answers will vary.

2. How many miles per hour faster is an average race car (200 mph) than the fastest skateboard?
   129.79 mph faster

3. Write your favorite way to roll down the street or sidewalk.
   Answers will vary.

7

Most Parachute Jumps in 24 Hours

Jay Stokes (USA) made 640 successful parachute jumps in 24 hours on September 8–9, 2006, in Greensburg, Indiana.

Did You Know?
Free fall occurs after skydivers jump but before they release a parachute. Gravity speeds the diver toward maximum velocity.

ACTIVITIES

1. About how many jumps did Stokes make each hour? Round to the nearest tenth.
   26.7 jumps per hour

2. Which part of skydiving would you enjoy most: jumping out of the plane, free falling, or floating back to Earth under a parachute? Explain your answer.
   Answers will vary.

8

Deepest Shipwreck

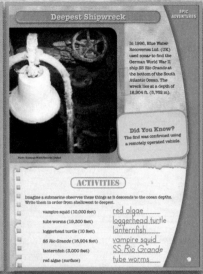

In 1996, Blue Water Recoveries Ltd. (UK) used sonar to find the German World War II ship SS Rio Grande at the bottom of the South Atlantic Ocean. The wreck lies at a depth of 18,904 ft. (5,762 m).

Did You Know?
The find was confirmed using a remotely operated vehicle.

ACTIVITIES

Imagine a submarine observes these things as it descends to the ocean depths. Write them in order from shallowest to deepest.

vampire squid (10,000 feet)   red algae
tube worms (19,300 feet)   loggerhead turtle
loggerhead turtle (10 feet)   lanternfish
SS Rio Grande (18,904 feet)   vampire squid
lanternfish (3,000 feet)   SS Rio Grande
red algae (surface)   tube worms

9

ACTIVITIES

1. Find Detroit, Michigan, and New York City, New York, on a map of the United States. To which city do you live closest? Estimate the number of miles between that city and yours.
   Answers will vary.

2. There are 0.62 miles in a kilometer. How many miles did Aguilar complete during this 1,000-kilometer adventure?
   a. 62
   b. 620
   c. 6,200
   d. 6.2

3. What was Aguilar's average speed in miles per hour? Circle your answer.
   more than 60 mph   less than 60 mph

4. What does trek mean?
   a. journey
   b. swim
   c. sleep
   d. interrogation

5. Find the average of the following numbers: 4, 10, 5, 6, 7.
   7

6. Aguilar completed the 1.24-mile course 500 times in about 10 hours. Complete the chart to show how many miles he had traveled at each hour mark.

Time in Hours	1	2	3	4	5	6	7	8	9	10
Mileage	62	124	186	248	310	372	434	496	558	620

11

Whip Cracking (Longest Whip)

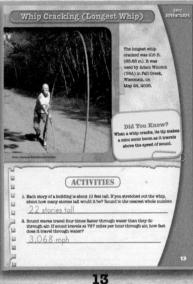

The longest whip cracked was 216 ft. (65.83 m). It was used by Adam Winrich (USA) in Fall Creek, Wisconsin, on May 24, 2006.

Did You Know?
When a whip cracks, its tip makes a mini sonic boom as it travels above the speed of sound.

ACTIVITIES

1. Each story of a building is about 10 feet tall. If you stretched out the whip, about how many stories tall would it be? Round to the nearest whole number.
   22 stories tall

2. Sound waves travel four times faster through water than they do through air. If sound travels at 767 miles per hour through air, how fast does it travel through water?
   3,068 mph

13

Highest Wall Climb on Darts

On November 11, 2009, Maiko Kiesewetter (Germany) reached a height of 16 ft. 5 in. (5 m) by climbing on darts.

Did You Know?
The first dartboards might have been cross sections of trees. The trees' rings may have inspired the rings on the modern dartboard.

ACTIVITIES

1. The word dart can be used as a noun and a verb. Write a definition for each word.
   dart (n.) a small, thin object with a sharp point
   dart (v.) to move suddenly and swiftly

2. If pairs of darts were embedded in the wall every nine inches, how many pairs would he need to reach 16 feet, 5 inches? Round to the nearest whole number.
   22 pairs of darts

14

Longest Platform-to-Platform Bicycle Jump

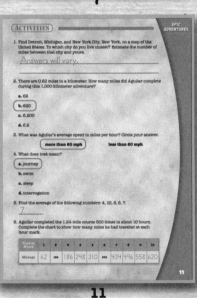

In 2009, Vittorio Brumotti (Italy) jumped 13 ft. 2 in. (4.02 m) from platform to platform on a bicycle in Milan, Italy.

Did You Know?
One easy bike trick is the bunny hop. Pull up on the handlebars to lift the front tire. Use your legs to lift the back wheel.

ACTIVITIES

1. With a friend, leap on the floor from pillow to pillow. How far can you spread the pillows apart and still make the jump?
   Answers will vary.

2. How far did Brumotti jump in inches?
   158 inches

3. If a bed mattress is 80 inches long, how many mattresses could Brumotti jump over? Round to the nearest whole number.
   2 mattresses

15

ACTIVITIES

1. How many people were included in the Tallest Tightrope Pyramid?
   a. 4
   b. 8
   c. 25
   d. 100

2. Build a pyramid with blocks or upside-down paper cups. How many levels tall can you make your pyramid?
   Answers will vary.

3. Do you think "The Flying Wallendas" makes sense as a nickname for this group? Explain why or why not.
   Answers will vary.

4. Fill in this pyramid. Each number should equal the sum of the two numbers below it.

   97
   46 51
   21 25 26
   10 11 14 12

5. Pretend you were at the circus during which The Flying Wallendas eventually got their name. Write an article about the event that would appear in the newspaper the next day.
   Answers will vary.

17

Largest Solar-Powered Boat

The MS Tûranor PlanetSolar (Switzerland) is 101 ft. 8 in. (31 m) long. It is covered with 5,780 sq. ft. (537 m²) of solar panels.

Did You Know?
Nine solar plants in California's Mojave Desert make up the largest solar thermal power generating plant in the world.

ACTIVITIES

1. In full sunlight, set one ice cube on white paper and one ice cube on black paper. Which paper absorbs the most heat from the sun and makes the ice cube melt faster?
   The black paper absorbs more heat, so the ice melts faster.

2. Would it be better to take a solar-powered boat trip during the summer or during the winter? Explain your answer.
   It would be better during the summer, when the sun shines more often.

18

Fastest Railed Vehicle (Rocket Sled)

EPIC ADVENTURES

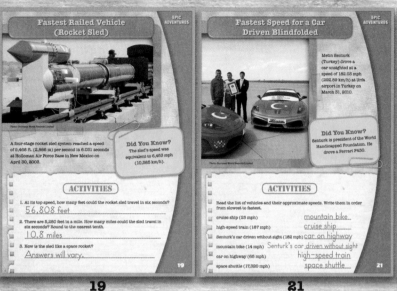

Photo: Guinness World Records Limited

A four-stage rocket sled system reached a speed of 9,468 ft. (2,886 m) per second in 6.031 seconds at Holloman Air Force Base in New Mexico on April 30, 2003.

Did You Know?
The sled's speed was equivalent to 6,453 mph (10,385 km/h).

ACTIVITIES

1. At its top speed, how many feet could the rocket sled travel in six seconds?
   56,808 feet

2. There are 5,280 feet in a mile. How many miles could the sled travel in six seconds? Round to the nearest tenth.
   10.8 miles

3. How is the sled like a space rocket?
   Answers will vary.

19

Fastest Speed for a Car Driven Blindfolded

EPIC ADVENTURES

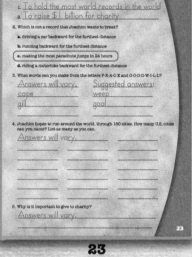

Photo: Guinness World Records Limited

Metin Senturk (Turkey) drove a car unsighted at a speed of 182.03 mph (292.89 km/h) at Urfa airport in Turkey on March 31, 2010.

Did You Know?
Senturk is president of the World Handicapped Foundation. He drove a Ferrari F430.

ACTIVITIES

Read the list of vehicles and their approximate speeds. Write them in order from slowest to fastest.

cruise ship (25 mph)   *mountain bike*
high-speed train (187 mph)   *cruise ship*
Senturk's car driven without sight (182 mph)   *car on highway*
mountain bike (14 mph)   *Senturk's car driven without sight*
car on highway (65 mph)   *high-speed train*
space shuttle (17,320 mph)   *space shuttle*

21

EPIC ADVENTURES

ACTIVITIES

1. What are two goals Joachim hopes to accomplish?
   1. *To hold the most world records in the world*
   2. *To raise $1 billion for charity*

2. Which is not a record that Joachim wants to break?
   a. driving a car backward for the furthest distance
   b. running backward for the furthest distance
   c. (making the most parachute jumps in 24 hours)
   d. riding a motorbike backward for the furthest distance

3. What words can you make from the letters P-E-A-C-E and G-O-O-D-W-I-L-L?
   Answers will vary.   *Suggested answers:*
   cape   *weep*
   gill   *goal*

4. Joachim hopes to run around the world, through 180 cities. How many U.S. cities can you name? List as many as you can.
   Answers will vary.

5. Why is it important to give to charity?
   Answers will vary.

23

Fastest Speed Barefoot Waterskiing (Female)

EPIC ADVENTURES

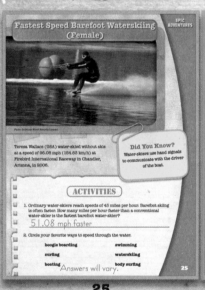

Photo: Guinness World Records Limited

Teresa Wallace (USA) water-skied without skis at a speed of 96.06 mph (154.53 km/h) at Firebird International Raceway in Chandler, Arizona, in 2006.

Did You Know?
Water-skiers use hand signals to communicate with the driver of the boat.

ACTIVITIES

1. Ordinary water-skiers reach speeds of 45 miles per hour. Barefoot skiing is often faster. How many miles per hour faster than a conventional water-skier is the fastest barefoot water-skier?
   51.08 mph faster

2. Circle your favorite ways to speed through the water.
   boogie boarding   swimming
   surfing   waterskiing
   boating   body surfing
   Answers will vary.

25

EPIC ADVENTURES

Longest Marathon on a Roller Coaster

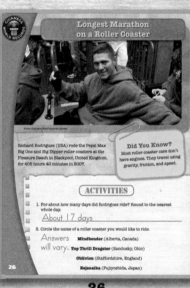

Photo: Guinness World Records Limited

Richard Rodriguez (USA) rode the Pepsi Max Big One and Big Dipper roller coasters at the Pleasure Beach in Blackpool, United Kingdom, for 405 hours 40 minutes in 2007.

Did You Know?
Most roller coaster cars don't have engines. They travel using gravity, friction, and speed.

ACTIVITIES

1. For about how many days did Rodriguez ride? Round to the nearest whole day.
   About 17 days

2. Circle the name of a roller coaster you would like to ride.
   Answers will vary.
   Mindbender (Alberta, Canada)
   Top Thrill Dragster (Sandusky, Ohio)
   Oblivion (Staffordshire, England)
   Eejanaika (Fujiyoshida, Japan)

26

Tallest Indoor Ice Climbing Wall

EPIC ADVENTURES

Photo: Guinness World Records Limited

An indoor climbing wall made of ice is in the O2 World Building in Seoul, South Korea. It stands 65 ft. 7 in. (20 m) tall.

Did You Know?
Ice climbers wear crampons (traction devices) on their feet. They kick into the ice, then swing an ax overhead to help them climb.

ACTIVITIES

1. Give the height of the tallest indoor ice wall in inches.
   787 inches tall

2. If each climbing step were 18 inches, how many steps would it take to climb the entire wall? Round to the nearest whole number.
   44 steps

3. If each 18-inch step took three minutes, how many hours would it take to reach the top of the wall?
   2.2 hours

27

ACTIVITIES

1. How long did Bradáč juggle three objects blindfolded?
   a. 15.26 seconds
   b. 20 seconds
   c. 25.30 seconds
   d. (47.26 seconds)

2. Draw a calendar for June of this year. Label dates correctly and include events that usually happen in June.
   Calendars will vary.

June						

3. Ask an adult to blindfold you as you get ready for bed at night. Then, complete the following activities without removing your blindfold. Which tasks were easy? Which tasks were difficult? Circle your answers.
   Answers will vary.
   Brushing your teeth   easy   difficult
   Washing your face   easy   difficult
   Putting on your pajamas   easy   difficult
   Climbing into bed   easy   difficult

4. Write about a time when your first attempt at something was unsuccessful. Did you try again? Were you successful on your second (or third) attempt?
   Answers will vary.

5. In your own words, explain the phrase "Practice makes perfect." Do you agree with this statement? Explain why or why not.
   Answers will vary.

29

EPIC ADVENTURES

Longest Motorcycle

Photo: Guinness World Records Limited

Colin Furze (UK) created the longest motorcycle, presented in Leicestershire, United Kingdom, in 2008. It was 46 ft. 3 in. (14.03 m) long.

Did You Know?
Up to eight standard motorcycles can fit in a parking space designed for one car.

ACTIVITIES

1. If a standard motorcycle is six feet (72 inches) long, about how many standard motorcycles would it take to match the length of the Longest Motorcycle? Round to the nearest whole number.
   8 standard motorcycles

2. Imagine riding the world's Longest Motorcycle. What are some problems you might have driving through town?
   Answers will vary.

30

Longest Time Breath Held Voluntarily (Male)

EPIC ADVENTURES

Photo: Guinness World Records Limited

Ricardo da Gama Bahia (Brazil) held his breath underwater for 20 minutes 21 seconds on September 16, 2010.

Did You Know?
Bahia hyperventilated with oxygen for 20 minutes 48 seconds before beginning the attempt.

ACTIVITIES

1. Twenty minutes is what fraction of one hour?
   $\frac{1}{3}$ of an hour

2. Humans breathe in air with oxygen and breathe out air with carbon dioxide. The chemical symbol for carbon dioxide is CO_2. What is the chemical symbol for oxygen?
   O

3. Can you hold your breath for 15 seconds? Circle your answer.
   yes   no
   Answers will vary.

31

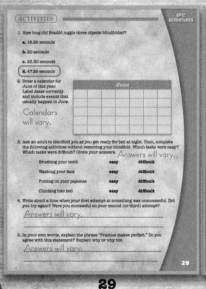

Most Consecutive Fire Flames Blown by Mouth (Without Refueling)

EPIC ADVENTURES

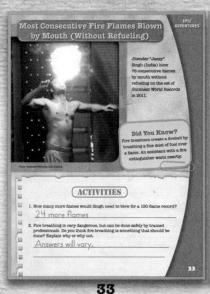

Jitender "Jassy" Singh (India) blew 76 consecutive flames by mouth without refueling on the set of *Guinness World Records* in 2011.

Did You Know?
Fire breathers create a fireball by breathing a fine mist of fuel over a flame. An assistant with a fire extinguisher waits nearby.

ACTIVITIES

1. How many more flames would Singh need to blow for a 100-flame record?
   24 more flames

2. Fire breathing is very dangerous, but can be done safely by trained professionals. Do you think fire breathing is something that should be done? Explain why or why not.
   Answers will vary.

33

33

ACTIVITIES

EPIC ADVENTURES

1. List three reasons why recycling is important.
   1. **It saves energy.**
   2. **It saves Earth's resources.**
   3. **It reduces the amount of waste in landfills.**

2. Could Bailey's crushing of aluminum cans with a monster truck be considered recycling? Explain your answer.
   Answers will vary.

3. Circle five words you read on page 34 to complete the word search. Use the word bank to help you.

paper glass plastic aluminum recycling

```
J N Y R C P O L R
R E C Y C L I N G
R T G A P A P E R
E A A F H T E D W
F D S N N I L K O
G O S L K C R F V
I A L U M I N U M
K H L F E S A W B
```

4. How many aluminum cans are used in your house each week? If 60 percent of those cans are recycled, how many are not recycled?
   Answers will vary.

35

35

Heaviest Aircraft Pulled by a Man

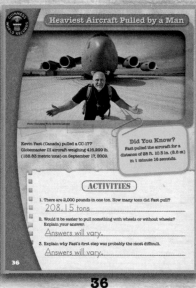

Kevin Fast (Canada) pulled a CC-177 Globemaster III aircraft weighing 416,299 lb. (188.83 metric tons) on September 17, 2009.

Did You Know?
Fast pulled the aircraft for a distance of 28 ft. 10.5 in. (8.8 m) in 1 minute 16 seconds.

ACTIVITIES

1. There are 2,000 pounds in one ton. How many tons did Fast pull?
   208.15 tons

2. Would it be easier to pull something with wheels or without wheels? Explain your answer.
   Answers will vary.

3. Explain why Fast's first step was probably the most difficult.
   Answers will vary.

36

36

Most Continuous Front Wheel Hops on a Bicycle

EPIC ADVENTURES

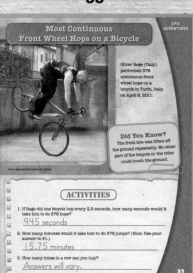

Oliver Rege (Italy) performed 378 continuous front wheel hops on a bicycle in Turin, Italy, on April 8, 2011.

Did You Know?
The front tire was lifted off the ground repeatedly. No other part of the bicycle or the rider could touch the ground.

ACTIVITIES

1. If Rege did one bicycle hop every 2.5 seconds, how many seconds would it take him to do 378 hops?
   945 seconds

2. How many minutes would it take him to do 378 jumps? (Hint: Use your answer to #1.)
   15.75 minutes

3. How many times in a row can you hop?
   Answers will vary.

37

37

Planet With the Most Moons

The planet Jupiter has 63 natural satellites. Most are small, irregularly shaped bodies of ice and rock.

Did You Know?
Saturn, with 61, has the second greatest number of moons.

ACTIVITIES

This sentence is a mnemonic device that can help you remember the order of the planets in our solar system: My very excellent mother just served us noodles. Write the names of the planets in order, starting with the planet closest to the sun.

1. **Mercury**
2. **Venus**
3. **Earth**
4. **Mars**
5. **Jupiter**
6. **Saturn**
7. **Uranus**
8. **Neptune**

38

38

Most Times to Take Off and Land in One Hour

EPIC ADVENTURES

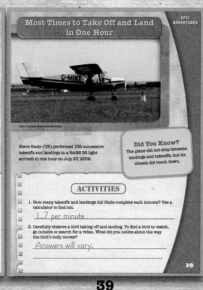

Steve Slade (UK) performed 102 successive takeoffs and landings in a RANS S6 light aircraft in one hour on July 27, 2002.

Did You Know?
The plane did not stop between landings and takeoffs, but its wheels did touch down.

ACTIVITIES

1. How many takeoffs and landings did Slade complete each minute? Use a calculator to find out.
   1.7 per minute

2. Carefully observe a bird taking off and landing. To find a bird to watch, go outside or search for a video. What did you notice about the way the bird's body moves?
   Answers will vary.

39

39

ACTIVITIES

EPIC ADVENTURES

1. Complete the crossword puzzle with words you read on page 40.

Across
4. A ski club in this country set the record for Most Water-Skiers Towed Behind a Single Boat.
6. You would need this to ski down a mountain.

Down
1. One type of waterskiing trick
2. Waterskiing is a _____.
3. Some people water-ski _____.
5. The club attempted to set the record _____ times before being successful.

```
      S  P  O  R  T
      N     U        B
4 A U S T R A L I A  A
      O     P        R
      W     I        E
      E           S  F
      V              O
      E  S  N  O  W  O
                     T
```

2. How many people were involved in setting the record for Most Water-Skiers Towed Behind a Single Boat?
   a. 25
   b. 4
   c. 7
   d. 114

3. Have you ever been snow skiing or waterskiing? Which would you rather do? Explain your answer.
   Answers will vary.

41

41

Most Concrete Blocks Broken in 30 Seconds

Ali Bahçetepe (Turkey) used his hands to break 655 concrete blocks in 30 seconds on November 11, 2009.

Did You Know?
Bahçetepe set another record the same day for breaking 1,077 concrete blocks in one minute.

ACTIVITIES

1. In Bahçetepe's first record, about how many blocks were broken each second? Round to the nearest tenth.
   21.8 blocks

2. Have a contest with a friend. Who can draw the most stars, circles, or other shapes in 30 seconds? Write the winning record.
   Answers will vary.

42

42

ACTIVITIES

EPIC ADVENTURES

1. If you owned a hot air balloon, what would it look like? Design it here.

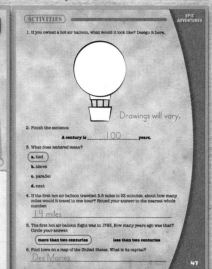

Drawings will vary.

2. Finish the sentence.
   A century is **100** years.

3. What does tethered mean?
   a. tied
   b. above
   c. parallel
   d. next

4. If the first hot air balloon traveled 5.5 miles in 23 minutes, about how many miles would it travel in one hour? Round your answer to the nearest whole number.
   14 miles

5. The first hot air balloon flight was in 1783. How many years ago was that? Circle your answer.
   more than two centuries   less than two centuries

6. Find Iowa on a map of the United States. What is its capital?
   Des Moines

47

47

Longest Time Spent Living Underwater

Richard Presley (USA) spent 69 days 19 minutes in a module underwater as part of Project Atlantis in Florida in 1992.

Did You Know?
The mission of Project Atlantis was to explore the human factors of living in an undersea environment.

ACTIVITIES

1. About how many weeks did Presley spend underwater?
   About 10 weeks

2. What do humans need that isn't found underwater? What would allow humans to survive underwater for a long time?
   Answers will vary.

48

Heaviest Vehicle Pulled With an Arm Wrestling Move

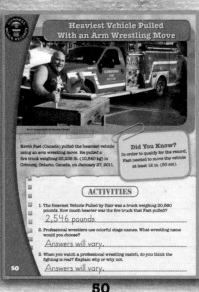

Kevin Fast (Canada) pulled the heaviest vehicle using an arm wrestling move. He pulled a fire truck weighing 23,236 lb. (10,540 kg) in Cobourg, Ontario, Canada, on January 27, 2011.

Did You Know?
In order to qualify for the record, Fast needed to move the vehicle at least 12 in. (30 cm).

ACTIVITIES

1. The Heaviest Vehicle Pulled by Hair was a truck weighing 20,690 pounds. How much heavier was the fire truck that Fast pulled?
   2,546 pounds

2. Professional wrestlers use colorful stage names. What wrestling name would you choose?
   Answers will vary.

3. When you watch a professional wrestling match, do you think the fighting is real? Explain why or why not.
   Answers will vary.

50

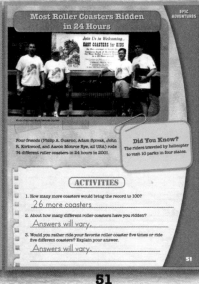

Most Roller Coasters Ridden in 24 Hours

Four friends (Philip A. Guarno, Adam Spivak, John R. Kirkwood, and Aaron Monroe Rye, all USA) rode 74 different roller coasters in 24 hours in 2001.

Did You Know?
The riders traveled by helicopter to visit 10 parks in four states.

ACTIVITIES

1. How many more coasters would bring the record to 100?
   26 more coasters

2. About how many different roller coasters have you ridden?
   Answers will vary.

3. Would you rather ride your favorite roller coaster five times or ride five different coasters? Explain your answer.
   Answers will vary.

51

ACTIVITIES

1. What is the normal human body temperature?
   a. 98.6°F
   b. 37°F
   c. 99°F
   d. 32°F

2. What is the freezing point for water in degrees Fahrenheit? Do some research if you need to. Circle your answer.
   more than 50°F   **less than 0°F**

3. What is your favorite thing to do in the winter? Draw a picture of it here.

Drawings will vary.

4. How much longer did Hof spend running a half marathon barefoot than he spent in full-body contact with ice?
   23 minutes, 52 seconds

5. If a half marathon is 13.1 miles, how long is a full marathon?
   26.2 miles

53

Fastest Half Marathon Wearing a Gas Mask

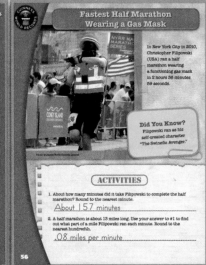

In New York City in 2010, Christopher Filipowski (USA) ran a half marathon wearing a functioning gas mask in 2 hours 36 minutes 59 seconds.

Did You Know?
Filipowski ran as his self-created character "The Swinefu Avenger."

ACTIVITIES

1. About how many minutes did it take Filipowski to complete the half marathon? Round to the nearest minute.
   About 157 minutes

2. A half marathon is about 13 miles long. Use your answer to #1 to find out what part of a mile Filipowski ran each minute. Round to the nearest hundredth.
   .08 miles per minute

56

ACTIVITIES

1. Why do you think it was verified that both aircraft weighed the same amount? What might happen if it had not been verified?
   Answers will vary.

2. What does victor mean?
   a. fan
   b. lead
   c. winner
   d. loser

3. Have you participated in any competitions? What kind? Write a story about what happened during your competition.
   Answers will vary.

4. Agarwal's time was 29.84 seconds. What was Joshi's time?
   a. 30.56 seconds
   b. 29.02 seconds
   c. 29.92 seconds
   d. 29.76 seconds

5. One meter equals 1.09 yards. How many feet did Agarwal pull the aircraft?
   327 feet

6. Agarwal beat Joshi's time by less than one second. True or false? Circle your answer.
   true   false

59

Largest Hiking Boot

Markus Appelman (Germany) made a boot that measures 23 ft. 5 in. (7.14 m) long, 8 ft. 2 in. (2.5 m) wide, and 15 ft. 9 in. (4.8 m) tall. It weighs 3,306.93 lb. (1,500 kg).

Did You Know?
The shoelace for this hiking boot is 114 ft. 9 in. (35 m) long and would stretch as high as a giant Ferris wheel.

ACTIVITIES

1. How much would a pair of the largest hiking boots weigh?
   6,613.86 pounds

2. Unscramble things you might see on a hike through the woods.
   rsirqul squirrel   dowrlifwl wildflower
   niep arte pine tree   teamor stream
   kawh hawk   meowad meadow

60

Greatest Distance on Theme Park Rides in One Hour

On September 14, 2003, Kerry-Ann Marshall (UK) traveled a total distance of 17,047 ft. (5,196 m) in 37 minutes on theme park rides at Thorpe Park, Chertsey, Surrey, United Kingdom.

Did You Know?
Thorpe Park is also home to the Colossus, a steel roller coaster that turns riders upside down 10 times!

ACTIVITIES

Why don't you fall out of your seat at the top of a loop on a roller coaster? Centrifugal force counteracts gravity and holds you in, even when you are upside down.

To see centrifugal force, do this experiment. Find a bucket with a handle and fill it ½ full of water. Go outside. Now swing the bucket by the handle in a wide loop, over and over. Describe what happens to the water.
Centrifugal force holds the water inside the bucket.

61

Tallest Rideable Motorcycle

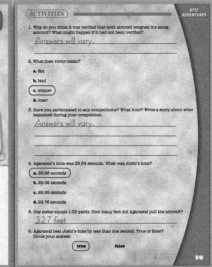

In 2005, Gregory Dunham (USA) built a motorcycle that is 20 ft. 4 in. (6.187 m) long and 11 ft. 3 in. (3.429 m) tall.

Did You Know?
The motorcycle weighs 6,500 lb. and is powered by an 8.2 L V8 engine. The tires are 74 in. tall.

ACTIVITIES

1. How many inches would the Tallest Rideable Motorcycle's tires reach over your head?
   Answers will vary.

2. Two thousand pounds equals one ton. How many tons does the motorcycle weigh? Use a fraction in your answer.
   3¼ tons

3. Where would you go on the world's Tallest Rideable Motorcycle?
   Answers will vary.

62

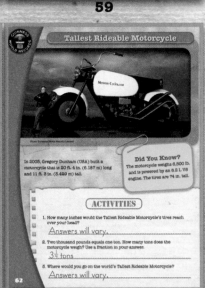

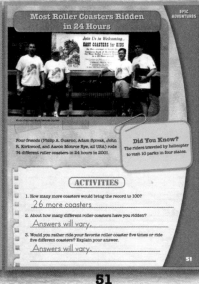

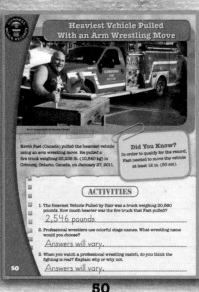

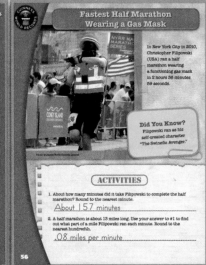

Fastest Jet-Powered Model Aircraft (Remote-Controlled)

A remote-controlled, jet-powered model aircraft created by Axel Haché (Dominican Republic) and David Shulman (USA) reached a speed of 293 Knots, or 337.16 mph (542.64 km/h) in 2010.

Did You Know?
The AMA (Academy of Model Aeronautics) certifies model plane flying records in the United States.

ACTIVITIES

1. Commercial jets fly at about 500 miles per hour. How many mph faster would the model jet need to be to reach this speed?
   162.82 mph faster

2. Knots measure the speed of ships and planes. A Knot equals 6,076 feet per hour. How many feet per hour is three Knots?
   18,228 feet per hour

3. Look at a map. What is the capital of the Caribbean nation the Dominican Republic?
   Santo Domingo

63

63

Fastest 100-Meter Bike Sled Race on Sand With Four Dogs

Four dogs pulled Susannah Sorrell (UK) 100 m in 11.65 seconds. The sprint took place in Holkham, Norfolk, United Kingdom, on November 6, 2007.

Did You Know?
Joe Redington is known as the "Father of the Iditarod." He raced in this famous dogsled race when he was 80 years old!

ACTIVITIES

1. Llamas help carry loads on steep climbs. Dolphins have been trained to locate underwater mines. Write three more ways animals help people.
   Answers will vary.

2. The Iditarod race ends each year in Nome, Alaska. Look at a map. Nome is on the coast of what body of water?
   The Bering Sea

64

64

Fastest 50-Meter Altitude Descent by Canoe

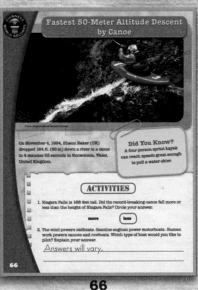

On November 4, 1994, Shaun Baker (UK) dropped 164 ft. (50 m) down a river in a canoe in 4 minutes 53 seconds in Snowdonia, Wales, United Kingdom.

Did You Know?
A four-person sprint kayak can reach speeds great enough to pull a water-skier.

ACTIVITIES

1. Niagara Falls is 168 feet tall. Did the record-breaking canoe fall more or less than the height of Niagara Falls? Circle your answer.
   more   less

2. The wind powers sailboats. Gasoline engines power motorboats. Human work powers canoes and rowboats. Which type of boat would you like to pilot? Explain your answer.
   Answers will vary.

66

66

Furthest Distance Skipping on a Rolling Globe

Katya Davidson (USA) traveled 2,008 ft. 4 in. (612.15 m) while skipping on a rolling globe that was 24 in. (60 cm) tall. She accomplished this feat at the Red, White, and Blue Parade in Citrus Heights, California, on June 26, 2005.

Did You Know?
There are colleges where you can earn a degree in circus variety arts, such as acrobatics, gymnastics, juggling, and clowning.

ACTIVITIES

1. Davidson set her record during a parade. What could you do in a parade to entertain the crowd?
   Answers will vary.

2. There are 5,280 feet in a mile. Did Davidson travel more or less than 1 mile? Circle your answer.
   less than ½ mile   more than ½ mile

3. How many times can you skip rope without stopping?
   Answers will vary.

68

68

Largest Snow Softball Tournament

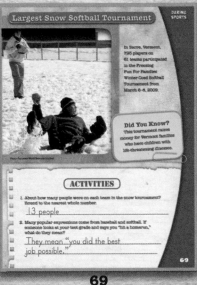

In Barre, Vermont, 795 players on 61 teams participated in the Freezing Fun For Families Winter Coed Softball Tournament from March 6-8, 2009.

Did You Know?
This tournament raises money for Vermont families who have children with life-threatening illnesses.

ACTIVITIES

1. About how many people were on each team in the snow tournament? Round to the nearest whole number.
   13 people

2. Many popular expressions come from baseball and softball. If someone looks at your test grade and says you "hit a homerun," what do they mean?
   They mean "you did the best job possible."

69

69

ACTIVITIES

1. Finish the sentence.
   A standard basketball weighs 22 ounces. Kettman was spinning a total of **38** pounds, **8** ounces when he broke the current record.

2. Make a time line of Kettman's life starting at the year he was born and including dates from the passage on page 70.

Kettman born	Age 4, Kettman begins spinning basketballs	Age 15, broke the record by spinning 10 balls	Broke the record by spinning 20 balls	Broke the record by spinning 28 balls
1972	1976	1987	1997	1999

3. If Kettman practiced an average of seven hours a day for 21 days, how many total hours did he practice to break his first record?
   a. 126
   b. 21
   c. 188
   d. 147

4. Kettman originally set the world record by spinning eight balls. True or false? Circle your answer.
   true   **false**

5. Set a goal for yourself. How many hours a day will you practice to achieve your goal? Give yourself a week of practice, then come back and write about your progress toward accomplishing your goal.
   Answers will vary.

71

71

Largest Returning Boomerang

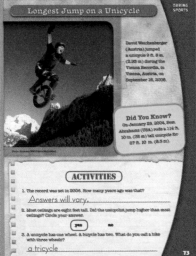

On July 1, 2008, Gerhard Walter (Austria) threw an 8 ft. 5 in. (2.57 m) boomerang at the University Sports Centre in Graz, Austria.

Did You Know?
The oldest known boomerang is 20,000 years old and was discovered in Poland.

ACTIVITIES

1. How many more inches would be needed for a nine-foot boomerang?
   7 inches

2. The word boomerang contains on. Write on to complete each word.
   st**on**e   s**on**
   d**on**e di**on**   h**on** vay
   b**on**d   r**on** star
   ball**on**s   s**on** s

72

72

Longest Jump on a Unicycle

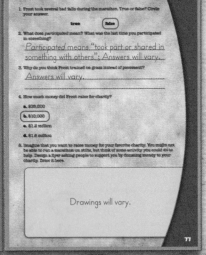

David Weichenberger (Austria) jumped a unicycle 9 ft. 8 in. (2.95 m) during the Vienna Recordia, in Vienna, Austria, on September 15, 2006.

Did You Know?
On January 29, 2004, Sem Abrahams (USA) rode a 114 ft. 10 in. (35 m) tall unicycle for 27 ft. 10 in. (8.5 m).

ACTIVITIES

1. The record was set in 2006. How many years ago was that?
   Answers will vary.

2. Most ceilings are eight feet tall. Did the unicyclist jump higher than most ceilings? Circle your answer.
   yes   no

3. A unicycle has one wheel. A bicycle has two. What do you call a bike with three wheels?
   a tricycle

73

73

ACTIVITIES

1. Frost took several bad falls during the marathon. True or false? Circle your answer.
   true   **false**

2. What does participated mean? What was the last time you participated in something?
   Participated means "took part or shared in something with others"; Answers will vary.

3. Why do you think Frost trained on grass instead of pavement?
   Answers will vary.

4. How much money did Frost raise for charity?
   a. $38,000
   b. $12,000
   c. $1.2 million
   d. $1.5 million

5. Imagine that you want to raise money for your favorite charity. You might not be able to run a marathon on stilts, but think of some activity you could do to help. Design a flyer asking people to support you by donating money to your charity. Draw it here.

Drawings will vary.

77

77

Furthest Distance on a Snowmobile on Water

DARING SPORTS

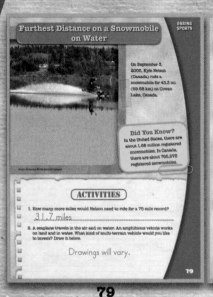

On September 3, 2006, Kyle Nelson (Canada) rode a snowmobile for 43.3 mi. (69.68 km) on Cowan Lake, Canada.

Did You Know?
In the United States, there are about 1.65 million registered snowmobiles. In Canada, there are about 705,575 registered snowmobiles.

ACTIVITIES

1. How many more miles would Nelson need to ride for a 75-mile record?
   31.7 miles

2. A seaplane travels in the air and on water. An amphibious vehicle works on land and in water. What kind of multi-terrain vehicle would you like to invent? Draw it below.
   Drawings will vary.

79

ACTIVITIES

DARING SPORTS

1. Draw a line of symmetry on the egg below.

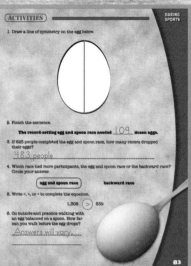

2. Finish the sentence.
   The record-setting egg and spoon race needed 109 dozen eggs.

3. If 825 people completed the egg and spoon race, how many racers dropped their eggs?
   483 people

4. Which race had more participants, the egg and spoon race or the backward race? Circle your answer.
   egg and spoon race   backward race

5. Write <, >, or = to complete the equation.
   1,308 (>) 839

6. Go outside and practice walking with an egg balanced on a spoon. How far can you walk before the egg drops?
   Answers will vary.

83

Highest Shallow Dive

DARING SPORTS

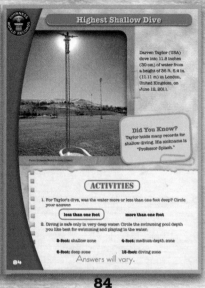

Darren Taylor (USA) dove into 11.8 inches (30 cm) of water from a height of 36 ft. 6.4 in. (11.11 m) in London, United Kingdom, on June 12, 2011.

Did You Know?
Taylor holds many records for shallow diving. His nickname is "Professor Splash."

ACTIVITIES

1. For Taylor's dive, was the water more or less than one foot deep? Circle your answer.
   less than one foot   more than one foot

2. Diving is safe only in very deep water. Circle the swimming pool depth you like best for swimming and playing in the water.
   2-foot: shallow zone   4-foot: medium-depth zone
   6-foot: deep zone   18-foot: diving zone
   Answers will vary.

84

Most Backflips on a Kick Scooter (Single Jump)

DARING SPORTS

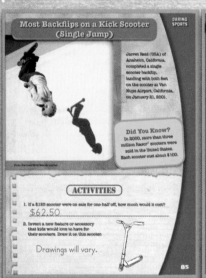

Jarren Reid (USA) of Anaheim, California, completed a single scooter backflip, landing with both feet on the scooter at Van Nuys Airport, California, on January 21, 2001.

Did You Know?
In 2000, more than three million Razor® scooters were sold in the United States. Each scooter cost about $100.

ACTIVITIES

1. If a $125 scooter were on sale for one-half off, how much would it cost?
   $62.50

2. Invent a new feature or accessory that kids would love to have for their scooters. Draw it on this scooter.
   Drawings will vary.

85

Greatest Distance by Pedal-Powered Boat in 24 Hours (Team)

DARING SPORTS

On May 7, 2005, the Trieste Waterbike Team (Italy) covered a distance of 110.3 mi. (177.3 km) in a pedal-powered boat in 24 hours in Trieste, Italy.

Did You Know?
Jason Lewis and Lourdes Arango (433.4 km) of the Timor Sea in 11 days in a 25-ft. (7.9-m) pedal-powered boat.

ACTIVITIES

1. What would you like to power by pedaling?
   Answers will vary.

2. How many more miles would the pedal-powered boat have to travel to reach 250 miles?
   139.8 miles

3. Make a boat from recycled materials you find, such as clean foam pieces and old containers. Write what you did.
   Answers will vary.

86

Highest Wall Ride on a Skateboard

DARING SPORTS

Brad Edwards and Aaron Murray (both USA) rode 7 ft. 6 in. (2.29 m) up a wall on their skateboards at the Hollywood Skate Jam in Hollywood, California, on August 25, 2005.

Did You Know?
Skateboarding first became an extreme sport in 1995 as part of ESPN's X Games.

ACTIVITIES

1. Geckos can climb walls easily using millions of tiny hairs, called setae, on the bottom of their feet. Where would you climb if you were a gecko?
   Answers will vary.

2. How many inches did the skateboarders ride up the wall?
   90 inches

3. Give one rule you know for skateboarding safely.
   Answers will vary.

87

ACTIVITIES

DARING SPORTS

1. An antonym is a word that has the opposite meaning of another word. Which is an antonym of descend?
   a. shout
   b. start
   c. ascend
   d. increase

2. What are two reasons why Innocente made his wild ride?
   1. To raise money for charity
   2. To prove that mountain bikes can go anywhere

3. Whose record did Innocente break?
   His own

4. Describe the challenges that Innocente faced as he rode down the underwater slope.
   He had to be careful of mud pools and large rocks in his path.

5. People should not go in the ocean and disturb the creatures there just to set a record. Do you agree or disagree with this statement? Explain your answer.
   Answers will vary.

6. Unscramble words you read on page 88.
   inygcle   cycling
   tduarerwae   underwater
   snounatia bkei mountain bike

89

Largest Sneaker

DARING SPORTS

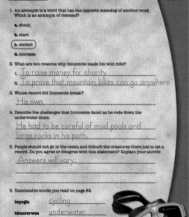

A sneaker measuring 13 ft. 1 in. (4 m) long, 5 ft. 3 in. (1.6 m) wide, and 5 ft. 7 in. (1.7 m) high was made on behalf of the UK's Race for Life. It was created in Cardiff, United Kingdom, in March 2009.

Did You Know?
The plastic tip at the end of a shoelace is called an aglet. If it wasn't there, we wouldn't be able to thread our shoelaces through the eyelets of our shoes.

ACTIVITIES

1. How many more inches would make the Largest Sneaker six feet high?
   5 inches

2. Is the Largest Sneaker longer or shorter than the room you are standing in right now? Circle your answer.
   Answers will vary.
   shorter   longer

3. What could a giant do while wearing giant sneakers?
   Answers will vary.

91

Most Soccer Balls Juggled

DARING SPORTS

Victor Rubilar (Argentina) juggled five regulation-sized soccer balls for 10 seconds at the Gallerian Shopping Centre, Stockholm, Sweden, on November 4, 2006.

Did You Know?
A regular soccer ball has 32 leather panels—20 hexagons and 12 pentagons.

ACTIVITIES

1. Which would be easier to juggle—scarves or soccer balls? Explain your answer.
   Scarves are lighter and have more surface area, so they are easier to grab.

2. How many times can you throw and catch a ball in 10 seconds?
   Answers will vary.

3. On what continent can you find Argentina?
   South America

93

Page 95

ACTIVITIES
DARING SPORTS

1. Which is closest to the speed of Boden's baseball pitch?
   a. a child skating
   b. a car traveling through a parking lot
   c. **a car traveling on a highway**
   d. a dog running in a park

2. How did Boden make history at her high school?
   She was the first girl to make the baseball team.

3. How much faster did the Fastest Softball Pitch travel than Boden's baseball?
   a. **3.9 mph**
   b. 4.9 mph
   c. 68.9 mph
   d. 66 mph

4. Round the speed of Mee's pitch to the nearest whole number.
   69 mph

5. Boden is one of a set of twins. True or false? Circle your answer.
   true   **false**

6. Play a game of catch with a friend. How many times can the two of you catch the ball without dropping it?
   Answers will vary.

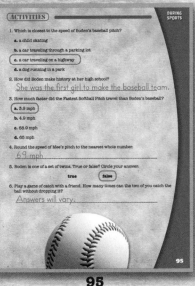

Page 96

Longest Somersault on Spring-Loaded Stilts

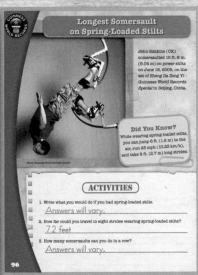

John Sunkins (UK) somersaulted 16 ft. 6 in. (5.04 m) on power stilts on June 18, 2009, on the set of Zheng Da Zong Yi - Guinness World Records Special in Beijing, China.

Did You Know?
While wearing spring-loaded stilts, you can jump 6 ft. (1.8 m) in the air, run 25 mph (10.25 km/h), and take 9 ft. (2.7 m) long strides.

ACTIVITIES

1. Write what you would do if you had spring-loaded stilts.
   Answers will vary.

2. How far could you travel in eight strides wearing spring-loaded stilts?
   72 feet

3. How many somersaults can you do in a row?
   Answers will vary.

Page 98

Most People Controlling Volleyballs

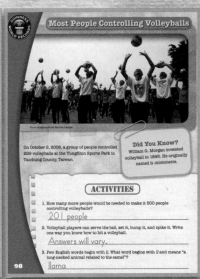

On October 2, 2008, a group of people controlled 299 volleyballs at the YungShin Sports Park in Taichung County, Taiwan.

Did You Know?
William G. Morgan invented volleyball in 1895. He originally named it mintonette.

ACTIVITIES

1. How many more people would be needed to make it 500 people controlling volleyballs?
   201 people

2. Volleyball players can serve the ball, set it, bump it, and spike it. Write one way you know how to hit a volleyball.
   Answers will vary.

3. Few English words begin with ll. What word begins with ll and means "a long-necked animal related to the camel"?
   llama

Page 101

ACTIVITIES
DARING SPORTS

1. What is an athlete? Why is Fotheringham a special kind of athlete?
   An athlete is "a person gifted in sports or physical contests"; Answers will vary.

2. Read the following statements. Circle true or false.
   Fotheringham was eight years old when he set his world record.
   true   **false**
   Fotheringham's nickname is "Flip."
   true   **false**
   Fotheringham performed his backflip in Los Angeles, California.
   true   **false**

3. What is Fotheringham's greatest pride?
   a. **his work with children**
   b. his world record
   c. his spins and jumps
   d. his athleticism

4. Fotheringham is a hero to both children and adults. Do you agree or disagree with this statement? Explain your answer.
   Answers will vary.

5. Write about a time when you overcame a difficulty in order to accomplish something that made you proud.
   Answers will vary.

6. Finish the sentence.
   Fotheringham is able to use his wheelchair like a skateboard because he practiced hard to learn

Page 103

Largest Soccer Ball
DARING SPORTS

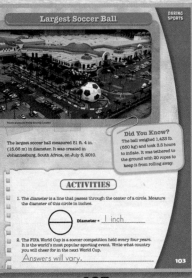

The largest soccer ball measured 51 ft. 4 in. (15.66 m) in diameter. It was created in Johannesburg, South Africa, on July 5, 2010.

Did You Know?
The ball weighed 1,433 lb. (650 kg) and took 3.5 hours to inflate. It was tethered to the ground with 20 ropes to keep it from rolling away.

ACTIVITIES

1. The diameter is a line that passes through the center of a circle. Measure the diameter of this circle in inches.
   Diameter = 1 inch

2. The FIFA World Cup is a soccer competition held every four years. It is the world's most popular sporting event. Write what country you will cheer for in the next World Cup.
   Answers will vary.

Page 104

Most Sacrifice Bunts in a Baseball Career

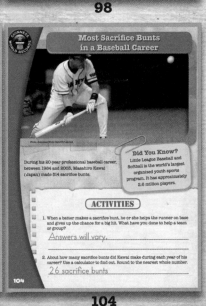

During his 20-year professional baseball career, between 1984 and 2003, Masahiro Kawai (Japan) made 514 sacrifice bunts.

Did You Know?
Little League Baseball and Softball is the world's largest organized youth sports program. It has approximately 2.6 million players.

ACTIVITIES

1. When a batter makes a sacrifice bunt, he or she helps the runner on base and gives up the chance for a big hit. What have you done to help a team or group?
   Answers will vary.

2. About how many sacrifice bunts did Kawai make during each year of his career? Use a calculator to find out. Round to the nearest whole number.
   26 sacrifice bunts

Page 105

Most Items Kicked Off People's Heads in One Minute
DARING SPORTS

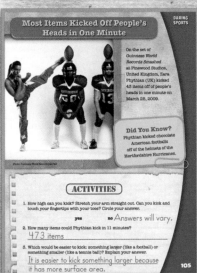

On the set of Guinness World Records Smashed at Pinewood Studios, United Kingdom, Zara Phythian (UK) kicked 43 items off of people's heads in one minute on March 28, 2009.

Did You Know?
Phythian kicked chocolate American footballs off of the helmets of the Hertfordshire Hurricanes.

ACTIVITIES

1. How high can you kick? Stretch your arm straight out. Can you kick and touch your fingertips with your toes? Circle your answer.
   yes   no   Answers will vary.

2. How many items could Phythian kick in 11 minutes?
   473 items

3. Which would be easier to kick: something larger (like a football) or something smaller (like a tennis ball)? Explain your answer.
   It is easier to kick something larger because it has more surface area.

Page 107

ACTIVITIES
DARING SPORTS

1. What is not another name for space hoppers?
   a. moon hopper
   b. **hip hip hop**
   c. kangaroo ball
   d. skippy ball

2. Finish the sentence.
   Space hoppers are made of rubber.

3. What does noteworthy mean? What is something noteworthy that has happened recently in your school or neighborhood?
   Noteworthy means "remarkable"; Answers will vary.

4. How much do you weigh? If a space hopper can support 600 pounds, how many people your size could fit on one? Circle your answer.
   five or more   less than five   Answers will vary.

5. Circle the animals that can hop.
   grasshopper   **kangaroo**
   elephant   **rabbit**
   zebra   koala

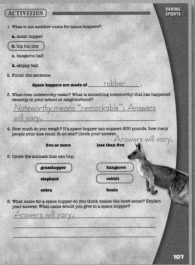

6. What name for a space hopper do you think makes the most sense? Explain your answer. What name would you give to a space hopper?
   Answers will vary.

Page 108

Longest Rideable Surfboard

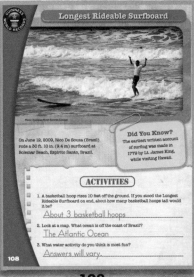

On June 12, 2009, Nico De Souza (Brazil) rode a 30 ft. 10 in. (9.4 m) surfboard at Bolemar Beach, Espírito Santo, Brazil.

Did You Know?
The earliest written account of surfing was in 1779 by Lt. James King, while visiting Hawaii.

ACTIVITIES

1. A basketball hoop rises 10 feet off the ground. If you stood the Longest Rideable Surfboard on end, about how many basketball hoops tall would it be?
   About 3 basketball hoops.

2. Look at a map. What ocean is off the coast of Brazil?
   The Atlantic Ocean

3. What water activity do you think is most fun?
   Answers will vary.

Card 109

Furthest Distance by a Hand-Cranked Cycle in 24 Hours (Male)

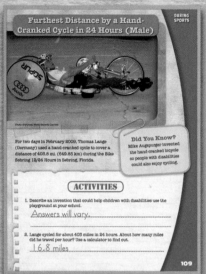

For two days in February 2009, Thomas Lange (Germany) used a hand-cranked cycle to cover a distance of 403.8 mi. (649.85 km) during the Bike Sebring 12/24 Hours in Sebring, Florida.

Did You Know?
Mike Augspurger invented the hand-cranked bicycle so people with disabilities could also enjoy cycling.

ACTIVITIES

1. Describe an invention that could help children with disabilities use the playground at your school.
   Answers will vary.

2. Lange cycled for about 403 miles in 24 hours. About how many miles did he travel per hour? Use a calculator to find out.
   16.8 miles

109

Card 113

ACTIVITIES

1. What is the relationship between Kimberly Mink and Cody Lamb?
   a. Mink is Lamb's sister.
   b. Mink is Lamb's aunt.
   c. Mink is Lamb's mother
   d. Mink is Lamb's neighbor.

2. Read the following statements. Circle true or false.

   Mink's family has talented performers.
   true   false

   Texas skip involves spinning a lasso.
   true   false

   Mink has an award for trick rope jumping.
   true   **false**

3. What does aptitude mean?
   a. dislike
   b. luck
   c. dull
   d. skill

4. Idaho borders six states. List those states here. Use a map to help you.
   1. Washington   4. Utah
   2. Oregon   5. Wyoming
   3. Nevada   6. Montana

5. Mink's family is a family of performers. Imagine that you and your family are performers. What might your family win awards for?
   Answers will vary.

113

Card 114

Fastest 100-Meter Hurdles Wearing Swim Fins (Individual, Female)

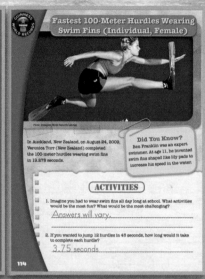

In Auckland, New Zealand, on August 24, 2009, Veronica Torr (New Zealand) completed the 100-meter hurdles wearing swim fins in 19.278 seconds.

Did You Know?
Ben Franklin was an expert swimmer. At age 11, he invented swim fins shaped like lily pads to increase his speed in the water.

ACTIVITIES

1. Imagine you had to wear swim fins all day long at school. What activities would be the most fun? What would be the most challenging?
   Answers will vary.

2. If you wanted to jump 12 hurdles in 45 seconds, how long would it take to complete each hurdle?
   3.75 seconds

114

Card 116

Longest Time Controlling a Soccer Ball While Lying Down

On November 24, 2007, Tomas Lundman (Sweden) controlled a soccer ball while lying down for 10 minutes 4 seconds at the Nordstan Shopping Mall in Gothenburg, Sweden.

Did You Know?
The elastic in Italian soccer player Giuseppe Meazza's shorts broke while he was taking a penalty shot during a semifinal match in the 1938 World Cup.

ACTIVITIES

1. How many times can you bounce a ball on your feet, hands, and body while you are lying down?
   Answers will vary.

2. For how many seconds did Lundman control the soccer ball?
   604 seconds

3. How many more seconds would be needed to set a record of 11 minutes?
   56 seconds

116

Card 117

Fastest 40 Meters by a Human Wheelbarrow

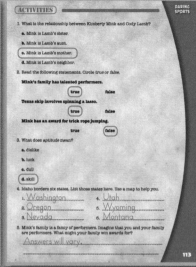

Adrian Rodriguez (Mexico) and Sergiy Vetrogonov (Ukraine) completed a 131.23 ft. (40 m) dash as a human wheelbarrow in 17 seconds. The record was completed in Helsinki, Finland, on November 12, 2009, in celebration of Guinness World Records Day.

Did You Know?
The Largest Human Wheelbarrow Race had 1,044 participants, or 522 pairs.

ACTIVITIES

1. Play human wheelbarrow with a friend. How many seconds does it take you to cross the room inside or cross the yard outside?
   Answers will vary.

2. Which do you like better—running on your hands as the wheelbarrow or running on your feet as the operator?
   Answers will vary.

3. About how far could the wheelbarrow team have traveled in one minute?
   462.60 feet

117

Card 119

ACTIVITIES

1. Dyrdek built the world's Largest Skateboard
   a. in his garage.
   b. on a playground.
   c. on his TV show.
   d. in Ohio.

2. Dyrdek began riding a skateboard when he was an adult. True or false? Circle your answer.
   true   **false**

3. In the passage on page 118, fantasy means "a product of the imagination." What would be an antonym of fantasy?
   reality

4. Skateboarding is a sport that requires riding on something. Name three other sports that require riding and tell what is being ridden.
   1. Answers will vary.
   2.
   3.

5. Design your own reality TV show. Tell what the show would be about and who would star in it.
   Answers will vary.

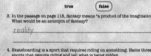

119

Card 122

Most Consecutive Skateboard Frontside Ollies (Half-Pipe)

On September 20, 2008, Keith Baldassare (USA) performed 348 frontside ollies (half-pipe) in a row in Merritt Island, Florida.

Did You Know?
Baldassare was only 13 years old when he achieved the record. He also raised $200 for the Grind For Life charity.

ACTIVITIES

1. What can you do 348 times in a row?
   Answers will vary.

2. The ollie skateboard trick was named after Alan "Ollie" Gelfand. What trick should be named after you?
   Answers will vary.

3. What is ⅓ of 348?
   116

122

Card 123

Most Overall Points Waterskiing (Women)

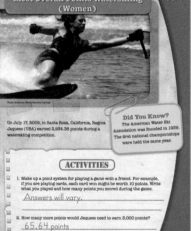

On July 17, 2009, in Santa Rosa, California, Regina Jaques (USA) earned 2,934.36 points during a waterskiing competition.

Did You Know?
The American Water Ski Association was founded in 1939. The first national championships were held the same year.

ACTIVITIES

1. Make up a point system for playing a game with a friend. For example, if you are playing cards, each card won might be worth 10 points. Write what you played and how many points you scored during the game.
   Answers will vary.

2. How many more points would Jaques need to earn 3,000 points?
   65.64 points

123

Card 124

Largest Snowboard

A snowboard measuring 32 ft. 9.7 in. (10 m) long and 7 ft. (2.15 m) wide was presented on March 18, 2007, in Flumserberg, Switzerland.

Did You Know?
Snowboarding combines surfing, skateboarding, and skiing. It first appeared at the 1998 Olympic Games with the giant slalom and the half pipe.

ACTIVITIES

1. One story of a building is about 10 feet tall. About how many stories tall is the Largest Snowboard?
   About 3 stories tall

2. Write snow to complete each compound word.
   snow man   snow suit
   snow cone   snow ball
   snow mobile   snow plow

124

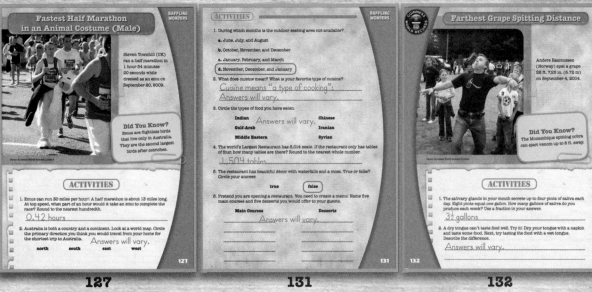

Fastest Half Marathon in an Animal Costume (Male) — 127

Steven Townhill (UK) ran a half marathon in 1 hour 54 minutes 20 seconds while dressed as an emu on September 20, 2009.

Did You Know?
Emus are flightless birds that live only in Australia. They are the second largest birds after ostriches.

ACTIVITIES

1. Emus can run 30 miles per hour! A half marathon is about 13 miles long. At top speed, what part of an hour would it take an emu to complete the race? Round to the nearest hundredth.
   0.42 hours

2. Australia is both a country and a continent. Look at a world map. Circle the primary direction you think you would travel from your home for the shortest trip to Australia.
   Answers will vary.
   north   south   east   west

ACTIVITIES — 131

1. During which months is the outdoor seating area not available?
   a. June, July, and August
   b. October, November, and December
   c. January, February, and March
   d. November, December, and January

2. What does cuisine mean? What is your favorite type of cuisine?
   Cuisine means "a type of cooking".
   Answers will vary.

3. Circle the types of food you have eaten.
   Indian   Chinese
   Gulf-Arab   Iranian   **Answers will vary.**
   Middle Eastern   Syrian

4. The world's Largest Restaurant has 6,014 seats. If the restaurant only has tables of four, how many tables are there? Round to the nearest whole number.
   1,504 tables

5. The restaurant has beautiful décor with waterfalls and a moat. True or false? Circle your answer.
   true   **false**

6. Pretend you are opening a restaurant. You need to create a menu! Name five main courses and five desserts you would offer to your guests.
   Main Courses   Desserts
   Answers will vary.

Farthest Grape Spitting Distance — 132

Anders Rasmussen (Norway) spat a grape 28 ft. 7.25 in. (8.72 m) on September 4, 2004.

Did You Know?
The Mozambique spitting cobra can eject venom up to 8 ft. away.

ACTIVITIES

1. The salivary glands in your mouth secrete up to four pints of saliva each day. Eight pints equal one gallon. How many gallons of saliva do you produce each week? Use a fraction in your answer.
   3½ gallons

2. A dry tongue can't taste food well. Try it! Dry your tongue with a napkin and taste some food. Next, try tasting the food with a wet tongue. Describe the difference.
   Answers will vary.

Largest Pack of Playing Cards — 133

The largest pack of playing cards measured 3 ft. 4 in. (101.6 cm) tall and 2 ft. 5 in. (73.6 cm) wide. The cards, made by Dan Bliss (USA), were displayed in 2005.

Did You Know?
A deck of playing cards can be randomized with five good shuffles.

ACTIVITIES

1. Give the height and width of each card in inches.
   40 inches and 29 inches

2. Multiply your two answers to #1. Give the area of each card in square inches.
   1,160 square inches

3. Divide your answer to #2 by 144 (or 12²). Give the area of each card in square feet. Round to the nearest tenth.
   8.06 square feet

Tallest Chocolate Fountain — 134

The tallest chocolate fountain is 26 ft. 3 in. (8 m) tall and circulates 4,409 lb. (2 metric tons) of chocolate at a rate of 120 quarts per minute. It is displayed in Las Vegas, Nevada.

Did You Know?
The ancient Mayans may have used chocolate as a form of currency.

ACTIVITIES

1. An average pitcher holds two quarts of liquid. How many pitchers of chocolate does the fountain circulate each minute?
   60 pitchers per minute

2. Give the difference between your height and the height of the fountain.
   Answers will vary.

3. What is your favorite chocolate treat?
   Answers will vary.

Largest Bottle of Cooking Oil — 135

The largest bottle of cooking oil stands 16 ft. 8 in. (5.12 m) tall and contains 706.54 gal. (3,212 L) of camellia oil. It was displayed in Guangdong Province, China, in 2009.

Did You Know?
The weight of the empty bottle was 4,801.8 lb. (2,178 kg).

ACTIVITIES

1. Over 1.3 billion people live in China. Write zeros in the spaces below to show this number.
   1,3 0 0, 0 0 0, 0 0 0

2. About ⅓ of China's population uses camellia oil, or tea seed oil, for cooking. How many people is this? (Hint: Use your answer to #1 and a calculator to find this very large number. Round to the nearest whole number.)
   185,714,286 people

3. What kind of cooking oil is used in your home?
   Answers will vary.

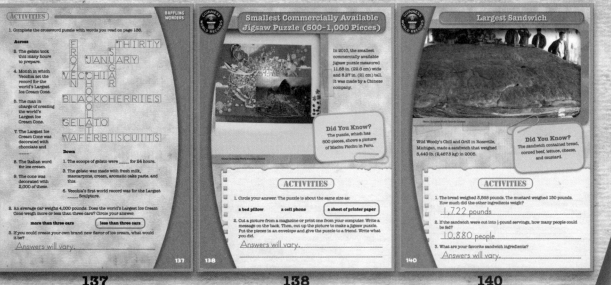

ACTIVITIES — 137

1. Complete the crossword puzzle with words you read on page 136.

   Across
   2. The gelato took this many hours to prepare.
   4. Month in which Vecchia set the record for the world's Largest Ice Cream Cone.
   5. The man in charge of creating the world's Largest Ice Cream Cone.
   7. The Largest Ice Cream Cone was decorated with chocolate and _____.
   8. The Italian word for ice cream.
   9. The cone was decorated with 2,000 of these.

   Down
   1. The scoops of gelato were _____ for 24 hours.
   3. The gelato was made with fresh milk, mascarpone, cream, aromatic cake paste, and this.
   6. Vecchia's first world record was for the Largest _____ Sculpture.

   Crossword answers:
   THIRTY
   JANUARY
   VECCHIA
   BLACKCHERRIES
   GELATO
   WAFERBISCUITS
   (Down: FROZEN, SUGAR, CHOCOLATE)

2. An average car weighs 4,000 pounds. Does the world's Largest Ice Cream Cone weigh more or less than three cars? Circle your answer.
   more than three cars   **less than three cars**

3. If you could create your own brand new flavor of ice cream, what would it be?
   Answers will vary.

Smallest Commercially Available Jigsaw Puzzle (500–1,000 Pieces) — 138

In 2010, the smallest commercially available jigsaw puzzle measured 11.65 in. (29.6 cm) wide and 8.27 in. (21 cm) tall. It was made by a Chinese company.

Did You Know?
The puzzle, which has 500 pieces, shows a picture of Machu Picchu in Peru.

ACTIVITIES

1. Circle your answer. The puzzle is about the same size as:
   a bed pillow   a cell phone   **a sheet of printer paper**

2. Cut a picture from a magazine or print one from your computer. Write a message on the back. Then, cut up the picture to make a jigsaw puzzle. Put the pieces in an envelope and give the puzzle to a friend. Write what you did.
   Answers will vary.

Largest Sandwich — 140

Wild Woody's Chill and Grill in Roseville, Michigan, made a sandwich that weighed 5,440 lb. (2,467.5 kg) in 2005.

Did You Know?
The sandwich contained bread, corned beef, lettuce, cheese, and mustard.

ACTIVITIES

1. The bread weighed 3,568 pounds. The mustard weighed 150 pounds. How much did the other ingredients weigh?
   1,722 pounds

2. If the sandwich were cut into ½-pound servings, how many people could be fed?
   10,880 people

3. What are your favorite sandwich ingredients?
   Answers will vary.

Card 143

1. Filling the Largest Bottle of Liquid Soap takes
   a. 90 minutes.
   b. 60 minutes.
   c. 45 minutes.
   d. 120 minutes.

2. Ask three friends or family members how tall they are. Then, add their heights together. Would they be shorter or taller than the Largest Bottle of Liquid Soap? Circle your answer. *Answers will vary.*
   shorter   taller

3. Unscramble words you read on page 142.
   marig — grime
   tuds — dust
   aewts — sweat
   thba — bath
   mpohsao — shampoo
   ohwesr — shower
   ecina — clean

4. Do you prefer taking baths or showers? Explain your answer.
   Answers will vary.

5. The average person uses 12.4 gallons of water to take a shower. Name a way you could use less water when taking a shower. *Suggested answer:*
   Answers will vary. Take shorter showers.

6. Find Saudi Arabia on a map. Name two countries that border Saudi Arabia. *Suggested answers:*
   1. Iraq, Jordan   2. Oman, Yemen

143

Card 144 — Largest Disco Ball

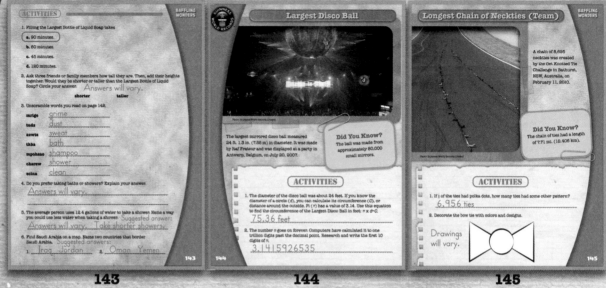

The largest mirrored disco ball measured 24 ft. 1.3 in. (7.36 m) in diameter. It was made by Raf Frateur and was displayed at a party in Antwerp, Belgium, on July 20, 2007.

Did You Know?
The ball was made from approximately 80,000 small mirrors.

ACTIVITIES

1. The diameter of the disco ball was about 24 feet. If you know the diameter of a circle (d), you can calculate the circumference (C), or distance around the outside. Pi (π) has a value of 3.14. Use this equation to find the circumference of the Largest Disco Ball in feet: $\pi \times d = C$.
   75.36 feet

2. The number π goes on forever. Computers have calculated it to one trillion digits past the decimal point. Research and write the first 10 digits of π.
   3.1415926535

144

Card 145 — Longest Chain of Neckties (Team)

A chain of 8,695 neckties was created by the Get Knotted Tie Challenge in Bathurst, NSW, Australia, on February 11, 2010.

Did You Know?
The chain of ties had a length of 7.71 mi. (12.406 km).

ACTIVITIES

1. If $\frac{1}{5}$ of the ties had polka dots, how many ties had some other pattern?
   6,956 ties

2. Decorate the bow tie with colors and designs.
   Drawings will vary.

145

Card 149

1. What is your favorite way to eat chocolate?
   Answers will vary.

2. The bar was 18.37 feet long, 9.02 feet wide, and 9.84 feet tall. True or false? Circle your answer.
   true   **false**

3. How long did it take to mix the chocolate glaze?
   a. 48 hours
   b. 43 hours
   c. 5 hours
   d. 53 hours

4. A candy company celebrates its 10th anniversary in 2010. In what year did the company start?
   2000

5. Circle five words you read on page 148 to complete the word search. Use the word bank to help you.

   chocolate cookies muffins brownies cakes

F	Z	P	M	D	I	X	Q	Q
L	C	B	T	C	X	Q	H	G
Z	A	R	M	M	W	K	D	J
K	X	O	W	W	C	C	E	V
R	T	W	H	C	O	O	K	I
T	X	N	E	H	O	C	Y	E
X	H	I	D	O	E	N	S	G
M	E	E	U	C	N	S	G	R
J	P	S	F	F	T	N	N	A
P	P	F	P	O	E	O	R	F
N	G	F	Y	C	X	K	D	S

   (words circled: CHOCOLATE, COOKIES, BROWNIES, CAKE, MUFFINS)

149

Card 150 — Heaviest Shoes Walked In

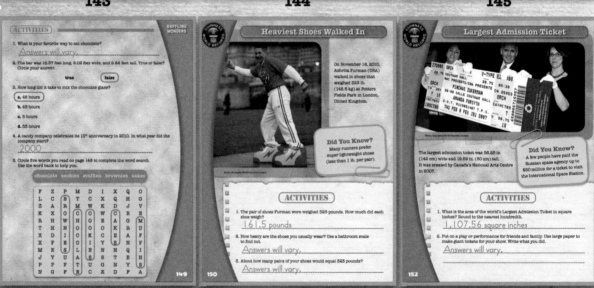

On November 18, 2010, Ashrita Furman (USA) walked in shoes that weighed 323 lb. (146.5 kg) at Potters Fields Park in London, United Kingdom.

Did You Know?
Many runners prefer super lightweight shoes (less than 1 lb. per pair).

ACTIVITIES

1. The pair of shoes Furman wore weighed 323 pounds. How much did each shoe weigh?
   161.5 pounds

2. How heavy are the shoes you usually wear? Use a bathroom scale to find out.
   Answers will vary.

3. About how many pairs of your shoes would equal 323 pounds?
   Answers will vary.

150

Card 152 — Largest Admission Ticket

The largest admission ticket was 56.25 in. (143 cm) wide and 19.69 in. (50 cm) tall. It was created by Canada's National Arts Centre in 2007.

Did You Know?
A few people have paid the Russian space agency up to $50 million for a ticket to visit the International Space Station.

ACTIVITIES

1. What is the area of the world's Largest Admission Ticket in square inches? Round to the nearest hundredth.
   1,107.56 square inches

2. Put on a play or performance for friends and family. Use large paper to make giant tickets for your show. Write what you did.
   Answers will vary.

152

Card 153 — Longest Ice Cream Dessert

The Kids Club (USA) in Brunswick, Georgia, prepared an ice cream sundae 130 ft. 6 in. (39.77 m) long on November 12, 2009.

Did You Know?
The sundae was made from vanilla ice cream, chocolate sauce, and peanuts. It weighed 169 lb. (76.7 kg).

ACTIVITIES

1. If the sundae were divided into six-inch servings, how many people could have some?
   261 people

2. The words *desert* ("a dry place") and *dessert* ("a sweet treat") are frequently confused. So are *sundae* ("ice cream with toppings") and *Sunday* ("the first day of the week"). Write definitions for these frequently confused words.
   piece a portion of something larger
   peace the absence of fighting

153

Card 155

1. Circle the toppings you would put on your perfect salad.
   tomatoes   croutons
   cucumbers   broccoli
   carrots   onions
   green pepper   shredded cheese
   bacon bits   peas
   Answers will vary.

2. There are many types of salads, such as macaroni salad and Caesar salad. How many more types of salads can you name? *Suggested answers:*
   potato salad   fruit salad   macaroni salad
   ham salad   taco salad   tuna salad

3. What was not done with the salad after the record attempt?
   a. It was given to locals.
   b. It was given to tourists.
   c. It was sold at markets.
   d. It was donated to shelters.

4. It took 700–800 volunteers to make the world's Largest Salad. True or false? Circle your answer.
   true   **false**

5. The world's Largest Pancake weighed 6,614 pounds when it was made in 1994. Which weighed more? Circle your answer.
   Largest Pancake   **Largest Salad**

6. Why do you think the salad was donated to shelters across Crete?
   Answers will vary.

155

Card 157 — Largest Box of Chocolates

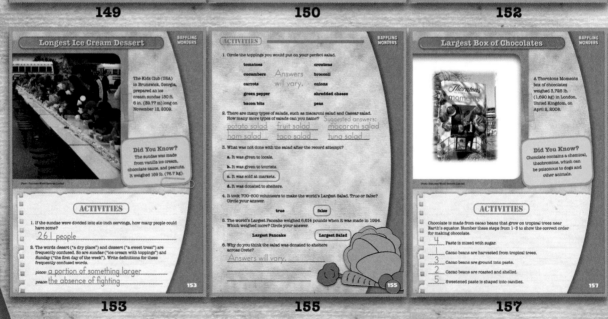

A Thorntons Momente box of chocolates weighed 3,725 lb. (1,690 kg) in London, United Kingdom, on April 2, 2008.

Did You Know?
Chocolate contains a chemical, theobromine, which can be poisonous to dogs and other animals.

ACTIVITIES

Chocolate is made from cacao beans that grow on tropical trees near Earth's equator. Number these steps from 1–5 to show the correct order for making chocolate.
   4 Paste is mixed with sugar.
   1 Cacao beans are harvested from tropical trees.
   3 Cacao beans are ground into paste.
   2 Cacao beans are roasted and shelled.
   5 Sweetened paste is shaped into candies.

157

Largest Muffin

The largest muffin weighed 195.55 lb. (88.7 kg) and measured 2 ft. 7 in. (79 cm) in diameter and 1 ft. 6 in. (45.8 cm) in height. It was made by master baker Gerhard Hinz (Germany) in 2010.

Did You Know?
The muffin contained wheat flour, butter, and lots of marshmallows.

ACTIVITIES

1. Circle your favorite muffin flavor.   Answers will vary.

   chocolate chip   banana nut   apple cinnamon
   carrot cake   blueberry   lemon poppy seed

2. Give the height of the Largest Muffin in inches.
   18 inches

3. The muffin used about 42 pounds of butter. How many ¼-pound sticks of butter were needed for the recipe?
   168 sticks of butter

159

159

ACTIVITIES

1. The record for the Longest Line of Pies was set in Ohio. True or false? Circle your answer.

   true   false

2. Is 530 feet of pies more or less than a mile? Circle your answer.

   more than a mile   **less than a mile**

3. If the average American eats six slices of pie per year, how many slices does the average American eat each month?

   a. one slice

   b. two slices

   c. 12 slices

   d. half a slice

4. The Longest Line of Pies consisted of 800 eight-inch pies. What is 800 multiplied by 8?
   6,400

5. Unscramble words you read on page 160.

   mpiunpk   pumpkin
   redssta   dessert
   khnavnigsTni Thanksgiving
   rtksuy   turkey

6. Describe your favorite Thanksgiving meal. What are your favorite things to eat on the holiday? Do you typically eat a slice of pumpkin pie?
   Answers will vary.

161

161

Largest Human Awareness Ribbon

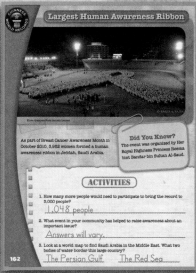

As part of Breast Cancer Awareness Month in October 2010, 3,952 women formed a human awareness ribbon in Jeddah, Saudi Arabia.

Did You Know?
The event was organized by Her Royal Highness Princess Reema bint Bandar bin Sultan Al-Saud.

ACTIVITIES

1. How many more people would need to participate to bring the record to 5,000 people?
   1,048 people

2. What event in your community has helped to raise awareness about an important issue?
   Answers will vary.

3. Look at a world map to find Saudi Arabia in the Middle East. What two bodies of water border this large country?
   The Persian Gulf   The Red Sea

162

162

Longest Line of Sandwiches

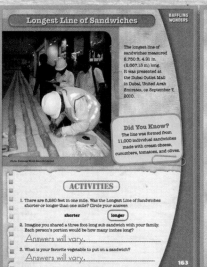

The longest line of sandwiches measured 8,750 ft. 4.91 in. (2,667.13 m) long. It was presented at the Dubai Outlet Mall in Dubai, United Arab Emirates, on September 7, 2010.

Did You Know?
The line was formed from 11,000 individual sandwiches made with cream cheese, cucumbers, tomatoes, and olives.

ACTIVITIES

1. There are 5,280 feet in one mile. Was the Longest Line of Sandwiches shorter or longer than one mile? Circle your answer.

   shorter   **longer**

2. Imagine you shared a three foot-long sub sandwich with your family. Each person's portion would be how many inches long?
   Answers will vary.

3. What is your favorite vegetable to put on a sandwich?
   Answers will vary.

163

163

ACTIVITIES

1. If each deck of cards cost $1.99, about how much money would Berg need to buy the cards for the Largest Playing Card Structure?

   a. $8,358

   b. $43,525.28

   c. $43,525

   d. $8,573.92

2. If Berg completed the structure on March 10, during which month did he begin building it? Circle your answer.

   January   February

3. What does replica mean?

   a. copy

   b. mistake

   c. original

   d. picture

4. Card games are fun. Do you agree or disagree with this statement? Explain your answer.
   Answers will vary.

5. Finish the sentence.
   China is on the continent of   Asia

6. China has people speaking almost 300 different languages. Do you know any words in another language? List as many as you can.
   Answers will vary.

167

167

Largest Slab of Fudge

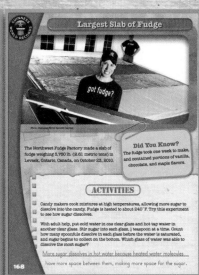

got fudge?

The Northwest Fudge Factory made a slab of fudge weighing 5,760 lb. (2.61 metric tons) in Levack, Ontario, Canada, on October 23, 2010.

Did You Know?
The fudge took one week to make, and contained portions of vanilla, chocolate, and maple flavors.

ACTIVITIES

Candy makers cook mixtures at high temperatures, allowing more sugar to dissolve into the candy. Fudge is heated to about 240° F. Try this experiment to see how sugar dissolves.

With adult help, put cold water in one clear glass and hot tap water in another clear glass. Stir sugar into each glass, ½ teaspoon at a time. Count how many spoonfuls dissolve in each glass before the water is saturated, and sugar begins to collect on the bottom. Which glass of water was able to dissolve the most sugar?

More sugar dissolves in hot water because heated water molecules have more space between them, making more space for the sugar.

168

168

Largest Beach Towel

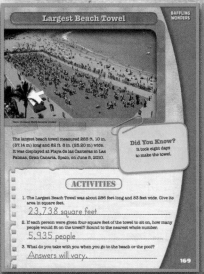

The largest beach towel measured 285 ft. 10 in. (87.14 m) long and 82 ft. 8 in. (25.20 m) wide. It was displayed at Playa de las Canteras in Las Palmas, Gran Canaria, Spain, on June 5, 2010.

Did You Know?
It took eight days to make the towel.

ACTIVITIES

1. The Largest Beach Towel was about 286 feet long and 83 feet wide. Give its area in square feet.
   23,738 square feet

2. If each person were given four square feet of the towel to sit on, how many people would fit on the towel? Round to the nearest whole number.
   5,935 people

3. What do you take with you when you go to the beach or the pool?
   Answers will vary.

169

169

Longest Chain of Shoes

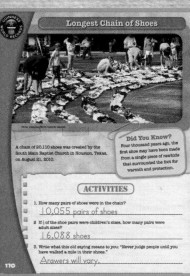

A chain of 20,110 shoes was created by the South Main Baptist Church in Houston, Texas, on August 21, 2010.

Did You Know?
Four thousand years ago, the first shoe may have been made from a single piece of rawhide that surrounded the foot for warmth and protection.

ACTIVITIES

1. How many pairs of shoes were in the chain?
   10,055 pairs of shoes

2. If ⅘ of the shoe pairs were children's sizes, how many pairs were adult sizes?
   16,088 shoes

3. Write what this old saying means to you: "Never judge people until you have walked a mile in their shoes."
   Answers will vary.

170

170

ACTIVITIES

1. Do you think the Largest Ant Farm habitat was effective in showing the importance of taking care of your teeth? Explain why or why not.
   Answers will vary.

2. Circle ways to take care of your teeth.

   eating healthy foods   eating sugary foods
   brushing your teeth twice a day   **visiting the dentist regularly**

3. Snacks that are low in sugar are the best options for keeping your teeth strong. What are three healthy snacks?

   a. apples, cake, and candy

   b. carrots, apples, and milk

   c. apples, carrots, and cake

   d. brownies, carrots, and milk

4. Explain the slogan "Just because you can't see it, doesn't mean it isn't happening."
   Answers will vary.

5. Do some research on Singapore and finish the sentence.
   Singapore is made up of   63   islands.

6. Create your own display that shows the importance of taking care of your teeth. Draw it here.

   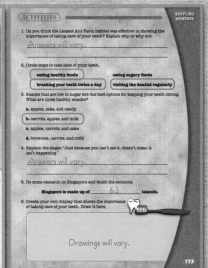

   Drawings will vary.

173

173

Largest Arcade Machine

The largest arcade machine measured 15 ft. 6 in. (4.14 m) tall, 9 ft. 4 in. (2.84 m) deep, and 8 ft. 8 in. (1.72 m) wide. It was unveiled in Los Angeles, California, on November 9, 2007.

Did You Know?
The arcade machine weighs 1,500 lb. (680.9 kg). It can play 150 different games.

ACTIVITIES

1. Estimate how many different arcade games or video games you have played in your lifetime.
   Answers will vary.

2. Write the names of your four favorite video games.
   Answers will vary.

3. If each game costs $0.50, how much would it cost to play all 150 games?
   _$75.00_

174

Largest Yo-Yo

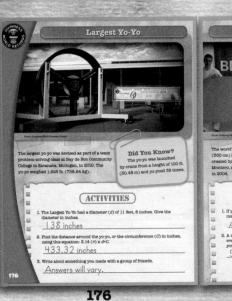

The largest yo-yo was devised as part of a team problem-solving class at Bay de Noc Community College in Escanaba, Michigan, in 2010. The yo-yo weighed 1,525 lb. (758.04 kg).

Did You Know?
The yo-yo was launched by crane from a height of 100 ft. (30.48 m) and yo-yoed 38 times.

ACTIVITIES

1. The Largest Yo-Yo had a diameter (d) of 11 feet, 6 inches. Give the diameter in inches.
   138 inches

2. Find the distance around the yo-yo, or the circumference (C) in inches, using this equation: 3.14 (π) x d=C.
   433.32 inches

3. Write about something you made with a group of friends.
   Answers will vary.

176

Largest Bandage

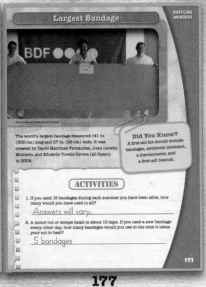

The world's largest bandage measured 141 in. (360 cm) long and 37 in. (95 cm) wide. It was created by David Martinez Fernández, Juan Lucero Montero, and Eduardo Torello Rivera (all Spain) in 2004.

Did You Know?
A first-aid kit should include bandages, antibiotic ointment, a thermometer, and a first-aid manual.

ACTIVITIES

1. If you used 15 bandages during each summer you have been alive, how many would you have used in all?
   Answers will vary.

2. A minor cut or scrape heals in about 10 days. If you used a new bandage every other day, how many bandages would you use in the time it takes your cut to heal?
   5 bandages

177

ACTIVITIES

1. Build your own sandwich! Circle the items you would put on your perfect sandwich.
   Answers will vary.

   turkey   cheese   mayonnaise
   relish   lettuce   ham
   tomato   onion   salami
   mustard   pickles   tuna

2. Using context clues, define mortadella.
   a. a type of bread
   b. another name for salami
   c. an Italian cold cut
   d. small sandwiches

3. Do you think setting a Guinness World Record would be easy to do? Explain why or why not.
   Answers will vary.

4. Circle five words you read on page 178 to complete the word search. Use the word bank to help you.

   bread sandwich salami mortadella tuna

B	S	A	N	D	W	I	C	H	F	V	T
O	A	X	A	D	N	K	H	R	G	I	U
N	L	Y	P	D	P	A	S	T	V	K	N
X	A	M	O	R	T	A	D	E	L	L	A
Q	M	O	F	I	M	K	M	X	H	G	V
W	I	Y	F	F	T	N	B	R	E	A	D

179

Longest Necktie

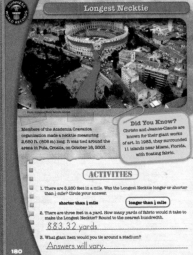

Members of the Academia Cravatica organization made a necktie measuring 2,650 ft. (808 m). It was tied around the arena in Pula, Croatia, on October 18, 2003.

Did You Know?
Christo and Jeanne-Claude are known for their giant works of art. In 1983, they surrounded 11 islands near Miami, Florida, with floating fabric.

ACTIVITIES

1. There are 5,280 feet in a mile. Was the Longest Necktie longer or shorter than ½ mile? Circle your answer.

   shorter than ½ mile   **longer than ½ mile**

2. There are three feet in a yard. How many yards of fabric would it take to make the Longest Necktie? Round to the nearest hundredth.
   883.32 yards

3. What giant item would you tie around a stadium?
   Answers will vary.

180

Heaviest Dog Breed

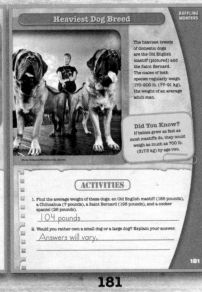

The heaviest breeds of domestic dogs are the Old English mastiff (pictured) and the Saint Bernard. The males of both species regularly weigh 170-200 lb. (77-91 kg), the weight of an average adult man.

Did You Know?
If babies grew as fast as most mastiffs do, they could weigh as much as 700 lb. (317.5 kg) by age two.

ACTIVITIES

1. Find the average weight of these dogs: an Old English mastiff (188 pounds), a Chihuahua (7 pounds), a Saint Bernard (196 pounds), and a cocker spaniel (25 pounds).
   104 pounds

2. Would you rather own a small dog or a large dog? Explain your answer.
   Answers will vary.

181

Tallest Costume Worn Running in a Marathon

In 2010, Jean Paul Delacy (UK) completed a marathon in London, United Kingdom, while wearing a giraffe costume measuring 23 ft. 1 in. (7.04 m) tall.

Did You Know?
Delacy finished the race ahead of a contestant carrying a giant mobile phone.

ACTIVITIES

1. Real giraffes stand up to 19 feet tall. How many inches taller was Delacy's costume?
   49 inches

2. What type of costume might help you run faster during a race?
   Answers will vary.

3. What type of costume might slow you down during a race?
   Answers will vary.

182

Largest Broom (Continental)

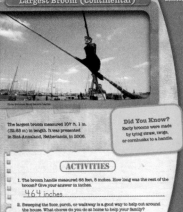

The largest broom measured 107 ft. 1 in. (32.68 m) in length. It was presented in Sint-Annaland, Netherlands, in 2006.

Did You Know?
Early brooms were made by tying straw, twigs, or cornhusks to a handle.

ACTIVITIES

1. The broom handle measured 68 feet, 8 inches. How long was the rest of the broom? Give your answer in inches.
   464 inches

2. Sweeping the floor, porch, or walkway is a good way to help out around the house. What chores do you do at home to help your family?
   Answers will vary.

183

Largest Dental Caps

Spike, a resident Asian elephant at the Calgary Zoo, Alberta, Canada, has dental caps that measure approximately 20 in. (50 cm) long, 5 in. (13 cm) in diameter, and weigh 29 lb. (13 kg) each.

Did You Know?
Some of the first toothbrushes were made with hair bristles from a pig's neck.

ACTIVITIES

1. What is the combined length of Spike's two dental caps? Give your answer in feet and inches.
   3 feet, 4 inches

2. Many wild elephants live south of the Sahara Desert. Look at a map. On what continent is the Sahara Desert?
   Africa

3. Do you know the answer to this elephant joke: What weighs 10,000 pounds and has glass slippers?
   Cinderelephant!

184
